NADIYA HUSSAIN

For Anne.
You are the cherry on the cake.

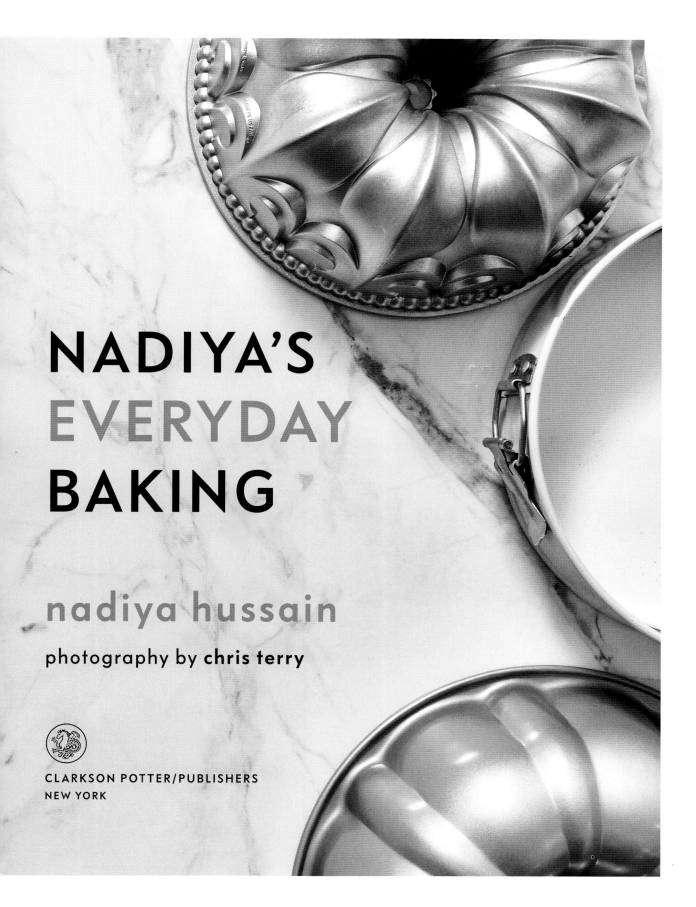

NADIYA'S
EVERYDAY
BAKING

nadiya hussain

photography by **chris terry**

CLARKSON POTTER/PUBLISHERS
NEW YORK

contents

HAPPY DAYS 112

BAKING DAYS 146

OUTDOOR DAYS 178

CELEBRATION DAYS 210

acknowledgments 248

index 249

introduction

Baking is a language I never imagined I would speak. As a first-generation British child growing up in a lively, colorful Bangladeshi home, bursting at the seams with delicious exotic food, we cooked everything, we ate everything; you name it, we ate it. We ate everything . . . but cake.

We didn't bake. We did stovetop cooking and reserved the oven space for storing frying pans and such. The oven knob untouched, never turned. It lay unused.

For some reason I never questioned it, why we never baked like Delia in her Christmas specials. She had an oven in the wall, whereas we had a free-standing one and despite my small, ever-inquisitive brain, I never questioned if they were the same thing: an oven, but just slightly different.

It was someone else's world. Not mine; well, not until it became mine.

Eventually I realized that anyone can bake, you don't have to have a fancy kitchen, an oven in the wall, expensive equipment, a TV show. Anyone can bake—

you, even me—all you need is an oven. You don't even have to love baking, as it's a love that grows with time, with every bake you undertake, and before you know it you'll be hooked on the sweet smell of baking in the kitchen.

Like me, you can learn to love baking with these straightforward, delicious, and achievable recipes. There is a recipe in here for every kind of day. Some days you might want cookies, cakes, or pastries, when you're relaxed and have time to spare. But other days you may be spending time outdoors, or in a rush during the week, and what you need is on-the-go food, or dinner on the table fast. There are also recipes for what I call rainbow days, when you want something healthier; days when you want to chill out with something cozy; and not forgetting those big celebration days. From surprise snickerdoodle cookies, an easy oven chicken stew, and a breakfast pizza, to angel layer cake slices, a whole citrus seabass, and a stunning meringue cake, who says you can't bake every single day?

chapter one
EVERYDAY KIND OF DAYS

banana and peanut butter roll-ups

Serves 8   Vegetarian

8 large flour tortillas

1¼ cups/320g crunchy peanut butter (or smooth if you prefer)

8 small or medium bananas

1 egg, beaten

7 tablespoons/100g unsalted butter, melted

6 tablespoons/ 75g sugar

½ teaspoon ground cinnamon

8½ oz/240g dark chocolate, chopped

⅔ cup/160ml boiling water

These are a winning breakfast and a great alternative to Saturday pancakes, using ingredients we commonly have at home: tortillas, peanut butter, banana. Rolled up, coated in sugar, and adorned with chocolate ganache, they are warm, crispy, and sweet. Let's just call them "end-of-the-week roll-ups" and we can have sweet feasts for breakfast all weekend long!

Preheat the oven to 400°F.

Onto the center of a tortilla, pop 1 heaped tablespoon of the peanut butter and spread from side to side to create a bed for your banana. Peel a banana and place on top. Make sure it sits in the center and is not sticking off the edge of the tortilla. If it is too long, break it to the right size (you can enjoy the extra bit as a light pre-breakfast snack).

Lift the flap of tortilla at each end of the banana and fold over. Lift the tortilla half closest to you and flap it over the banana. Now hold it firmly and roll just till you get to the end. Brush the end with the egg and finish rolling, then place seam-side down so the egg and tortilla can stick, making sure the delicious contents do not escape easily. Pop onto a baking sheet and do the remaining seven.

Brush the melted butter all over the rolls, turning them around till you have covered them all. Place them seam-side down. You will have leftover butter, not a lot, but set that aside as you will need it a little later. Bake in the oven for 8 minutes, till crisp and golden all over.

Meanwhile, mix the sugar and cinnamon on a large baking sheet or plate.

Take the rolls out and switch the broiler on to high heat.

Using the leftover butter, brush all over the rolls till you have no more butter left. Using a pair of tongs, carefully roll the roll-ups till they are coated in the sugar and put back on the baking sheet till you have done all eight.

Place under the broiler for 1 minute. Don't walk away as it will only take 50 seconds to 1 minute before you get a beautiful brûléed top. Keep an eye on it and as soon as it's golden on top and shiny, it's ready. Take out and let that caramelized sugar set to a deep crunch.

Melt the chocolate by putting the chopped pieces in a bowl, pouring in the boiling water, and mixing, agitating and moving the mixture till you have a glossy ganache. You can serve this as a dipping sauce on the side, but I like to generously swish the ganache right on top of the roll-ups and eat them while they are warm.

harissa
pita pockets

6 large pitas

⅔ cup/120g rose harissa paste (or regular harissa paste)

6 large eggs

3 small or medium avocados

a pinch of ground cumin

honey, for drizzling

| Serves 6 | Vegetarian |

This recipe is designed to use all the things that I have knocking around the house. Simple, delicious pastes (like the harissa in this recipe), a carb (I always have pita in the pantry or the freezer), and let's not forget the eggs! Put them all together and top with avocado and you have a quick, easy, and totally different take on avocado toast.

Preheat the oven to 400°F. Have a baking sheet ready that fits all six of the pitas comfortably.

Lay the pitas out on the baking sheet. Mix the jar of harissa so the oil and paste are mixed well, as sometimes through settling the oil and paste separate. Spread a small spoonful of the paste all over each pita, turning each around to spread evenly on both sides.

Pop into the oven for 5½ minutes, or till the pitas are crisp on the outside and puffed right up, creating a pouch.

Take out of the oven and, using scissors or a knife, create a 1-inch/2.5cm slit in each pita. Break 1 egg into a bowl and pour into each pita, holding the slit open using a spoon.

Pop back in the oven for 1½ minutes for a runny yolk or, if you would like a firm yolk (as does my husband because he believes a runny yolk is the work of the devil), then bake them for 3 minutes.

Slice up half an avocado for each pita, pop the slices on top of the harissa pitas, sprinkle with the cumin, and finish with a generous drizzle of honey.

keema sheet pan panini

Serves 6

1 teaspoon olive oil

8 oz/220g ground lamb

⅓ cup/25g crispy fried onions

1 tablespoon garlic and ginger paste

½ teaspoon salt

1 teaspoon chile flakes

2 teaspoons garam masala

a small handful of cilantro, chopped

5¾ oz/160g queso fresco, chopped or crumbled

5 tablespoons/70g siracha mayo

½ cup/125g garlic butter, melted

2½ oz/75g cheddar cheese, finely grated (⅔ cup)

6 slices of cheddar cheese

12 slices of white bread

My kids love panini, but I hate taking the panini machine thingy out of the cupboard. I have three kids, two of which are always ravenous, and one who eats a tiny amount and then comes back looking for the leftovers later. And as much as I love being in the kitchen, I also love doing other things. So, these are for the rushed among us—they're all-in-one and delicious, with spiced meat and jalapeño cheese.

Start by adding the oil to a nonstick frying pan. Pop onto high heat and as soon as the oil is hot, add the lamb and fry till it's cooked through and brown. As soon as it is ready, use a slotted spoon to transfer the mixture to a large bowl, draining off any excess oil.

To the cooked lamb, add the crispy fried onions, garlic and ginger paste, salt, chile flakes, garam masala, and chopped cilantro and mix well. Add the queso fresco and mayo and mix again. You will have a mixture that really holds its shape.

Preheat the oven to 350°F and have a nonstick or lined baking sheet at the ready, large enough to fit six slices of bread. Grease the inside of the sheet with some of the garlic butter and sprinkle with the grated cheddar. Set aside.

Spread the lamb mixture evenly onto six slices of bread, spreading all the way to the edges. Add 1 slice of cheddar on top of each and then another slice of bread on top. Press down firmly so all the layers really stick together.

Brush both sides with garlic butter and lay on top of the grated cheese in the baking sheet, then brush all over with any leftover garlic butter. Pop another sheet right on top of the sandwiches. I then like to take a roasting dish or something similarly heavy and pop that on top to help weigh it down.

Now bake for 15 minutes till crisp. Once they are out, let cool on the sheet for 5 minutes; you should have crisp cheese on the outside and gooey cheese in the middle.

It's okay to have panini for breakfast, lunch, and dinner, but at least this way you're not there spatulating panini for days! Enjoy! →

potato peel chips

Serves 4–6   Vegetarian/Gluten-free

¼ cup/60ml olive oil

3 large egg whites

10½ oz/300g potato peelings (the peel of approx. 12 medium potatoes, depending on size)

1¼ cups/110g chickpea flour (gram flour), sifted

2 tablespoons onion granules

1 tablespoon garlic granules

1 tablespoon black sesame seeds

1½ teaspoons chile powder

1½ teaspoons fine salt

sea salt flakes

I like nothing more than reducing waste, so if I'm peeling potatoes, then we are also having potato peel chips. To think these might have spent their final days in a compost bin, when instead they can be turned into a crisp, spiced, tempting snack, perfect when having people over, or just for everyday nibbling if you are a nibbler like me.

Preheat the oven to 400°F. Have two large baking sheets at the ready, drizzle the oil in, and pop into the oven for the oil to heat up.

Put the egg whites in a large bowl and whisk till they are light and fluffy. We are not looking for a meringue-type texture, just frothy and fluffy and increased in volume. Take the potato peelings and add to the egg white bowl. Using your hands, get all that frothy mixture to coat all the peel pieces.

In another bowl, combine the chickpea flour, onion granules, garlic granules, sesame seeds, chile, and fine salt and give everything a really good mix, making sure to remove any lumps of flour. Sprinkle this all over the peel and egg mixture and then use two forks to distribute the mixture so everything gets a coating.

Take the hot sheets out of the oven and pop the peel mixture on in lumps. Use your fork to spread out into a thin layer. Bake for 15 minutes, then remove from the oven and, using a fork, turn the mixture, loosening any large clumps, then bake again for 6 minutes, till crisp. Repeat this step with any uncooked peel until it's all crisp and dry.

Take out, sprinkle with sea salt flakes, and let cool on the sheet to really crisp up. Once cool enough, tumble into a bowl. It's perfect as a side dish or snack—no waste and delicious!

jam layer flapjacks

1 cup plus 2 tablespoons/250g unsalted butter

½ cup/120ml golden syrup or light corn syrup

¾ cup plus 2 tablespoons/180g sugar

oil, for greasing

5½ cups/500g rolled oats

2 teaspoons almond extract

⅔ cup/200g raspberry jam

For the topping

1¾ oz/50g dark chocolate, chopped

1¾ oz/50g milk chocolate, chopped

1¾ oz/50g white chocolate, chopped

Serves 12   Vegetarian/Gluten-free

Nothing says I love you like a flapjack from the gas station after filling up the car. At least, that's my interpretation of what love is! My husband, Abdal, knows it, as I always have a stash of Bakewell imitation flapjacks that sit in my bag for when hunger strikes. These are exactly like those: buttery sweet with a tart layer of fruit running right through the center and topped off with a marbled trio of chocolate.

Put the butter, golden syrup, and sugar in a pan and pop onto low heat. Stir occasionally, encouraging the butter and sugar to melt.

Preheat the oven to 350°F. Line and grease an 8-inch/20cm square baking pan and set aside. Be sure to leave some paper overhanging to make it easier to lift the flapjack out.

Put the oats in a large bowl. Add the almond extract to the melted butter mixture and stir well. Pour the mixture all over the oats and mix well till you no longer have any patches of dry oats.

Take half the mixture and press firmly into the pan, getting it into every corner. Make sure you have an even layer. Spread the jam in a thin layer, evenly distributing it across the oat mixture.

Top with the other half of the oat mixture, again using the back of a spoon to spread the mixture all over in an even layer, being a bit gentler this time so as not to agitate the jam layer. Pop into the oven to bake for 30 minutes.

The flapjack will be golden around the edge but not fully set in the center when you take it out. Pop onto a cooling rack still in its pan.

Take the three types of chocolate and mix the pieces in a bowl, so the three colors are distributed. Sprinkle all over the hot flapjack and set aside for 10–12 minutes, till the chocolate is glossy and melted. Use the back of a spoon or an offset spatula to just smooth and ripple the top.

Let cool and set completely. Lift out of the pan, cut into 12 equal squares, and they are ready to eat, or to pack into your handbag till hunger strikes. Because it will!

whole roasted onion curry

Serves 4   Vegetarian/Gluten-free

¼ cup/50g clarified butter (ghee)

5 onions, halved

1 teaspoon salt

For the sauce

5 cloves of garlic

6 tomatoes, peeled and chopped

1 tablespoon tomato paste

2 tablespoons tamarind paste

1 teaspoon salt

1 tablespoon curry powder

1 teaspoon chile powder

To serve

basmati rice

fresh cilantro

heavy cream

Onions are the starter of every good dish; without them, there is often no base, no sweetness, no foundation. But for once let's allow the allium to be the main star of the show. When cooked gently, onions are sweet, and here they are roasted to perfection and baked in a simple sauce for a curry that's conveniently all done in the oven.

Start by preheating the oven to 400°F. Take a large Dutch oven (with a lid) that's big enough to comfortably hold the onions.

Add the clarified butter to the Dutch oven and pop onto the stove to melt the butter. As soon as it's smoking hot, add the onions, flat-side down. They should sizzle. Sprinkle with salt. Let the onions cook for 5 minutes. Once all the onions have sizzled, pop into the oven and roast for 20 minutes.

Make the quick curry base by combining the garlic, peeled tomatoes, tomato paste, tamarind, and salt in a food processor. Add the curry and chile powders and blitz to a smooth paste.

Take the onions out of the oven and lower the heat to 350°F. Flip the onions over onto their rounded sides.

Pour the curry mixture in and around the onions, put the lid on, and place back in the oven to cook gently for 25 minutes.

Meanwhile, cook the rice and chop the cilantro.

Take the dish out of the oven and remove the lid. Drizzle the cream, sprinkle with some cilantro, and it's ready to dig into.

sweet potato jalapeño gratin

Serves 4–6   Vegetarian/Gluten-free

1 lb 7 oz/650g sweet potatoes

1 tablespoon lemon juice

1 quart/1 liter boiling water

butter, for greasing

1¼ cups/300ml heavy cream

2 cloves of garlic

½ teaspoon salt

1¾ oz/50g extra-mature cheddar cheese, grated

For the sauce

2–3 fresh jalapeños, seeded if you like it less spicy

⅓ cup/7g fresh mint

pinch of salt

¼ cup/60ml olive oil

4 teaspoons lemon juice

2 teaspoons honey

I never used to be a huge fan of sweet potato, torn between "is it a carrot?" or "is it a potato?" Either way, it turns out it is a wonderful ingredient, which when made simply and adorned well, can taste phenomenal. This is one such example, in which sweet, creamy, garlicky potatoes are drizzled with a fresh jalapeño and mint sauce.

Peel the sweet potatoes and then cut into thin slices lengthwise. Pop into a large bowl, add the lemon juice, and then pour in the boiling water. Let the sweet potato gently cook in the bowl.

Grease the bottom and sides of a 10-inch/25cm roasting dish. Drain the sweet potato after 10 minutes and rinse under cold water.

Take the slices of potato and place them lined up in a row in the dish, continuing to do so till you fill up the dish, placing each row next to another and making sure to fill in all the gaps and slits.

Preheat the oven to 375°F.

Pop the cream into a pan, mince the garlic into the cream, and add a pinch of salt. As soon as the cream comes to a boil, take it off the heat and pour it all over the sweet potato slices in the dish. Sprinkle with the cheese and bake for 30 minutes.

Meanwhile, make the sauce by putting the jalapeños, mint leaves, salt, oil, lemon juice, and honey into a bowl and using an immersion blender to blitz to a smooth sauce.

As soon as the gratin comes out of the oven, drizzle with the sauce and it is ready to serve while hot. Any leftover sauce can be served on the side for anyone who wants some more. This is perfect as a side to a delicious roasted chicken or it's equally delicious as a dip.

crispy tofu lettuce wraps

Serves 12–14

2 tablespoons sunflower oil

1 lb/450g firm tofu

12–14 leaves of little gem lettuce

1 small red onion, thinly sliced

a handful of fresh cilantro, chopped

1 large red chile, thinly sliced

juice of ½ lime

For the marinade

2 teaspoons yeast extract, such as Marmite or Vegemite

1 meat-free beef or beef stock cube

2 tablespoons sunflower oil

1 tablespoon garlic and ginger paste

For the sauce

6 tablespoons/100g smooth peanut butter

2 tablespoons chile oil

It has taken this recipe to finally get my kids to like tofu. Although they aren't usually fussy, when they say they don't like a food, it quite literally becomes my life's mission to do something, anything, everything to it to get them to change their mind; even an "it's okay" will suffice. And this recipe is more than okay: they love these wraps and devour them, and "can we have that again?" are words I do like to hear. This crispy, crumbled tofu has an earthy meaty flavor. I've combined it with crunchy onions and a peanut sauce, all wrapped in a crisp lettuce leaf.

Start by preheating the oven to 400°F. Drizzle the oil over a large baking sheet.

Take the block of tofu and pat dry, squeezing with some paper towels to remove any excess moisture. Crumble the tofu into the baking sheet till you have pieces that are the size of ground meat when cooked. Spread out in an even layer and bake for 12–15 minutes to start to crisp it up and remove some moisture.

Now make the "meat" flavor marinade by combining the yeast extract, stock cube, oil, and ginger and garlic paste and giving it a really good mix.

Take the tofu out of the oven, add the marinade and, using a spoon, give it all a mix till every bit of the tofu is covered in that marinade, then pop it back in the oven for 10 minutes. It should be looking and smelling more like cooked meat.

Make the sauce by mixing the peanut butter and chile oil to an even mixture. Lay the lettuce leaves on a plate.

Take the tofu out of the oven, add the sliced onion, cilantro, and chile and mix well. The heat of the tofu will really soften the zing of the raw onion. Spoon the mixture into the lettuce leaves, drizzle with the peanut sauce, squeeze on the lime juice, and your lettuce wraps are ready to share and enjoy.

→

salmon moussaka

5 medium eggplant, cut into ½-inch/1cm slices (prepped weight 2½ lb/1.2kg)

7 tablespoons/100ml olive oil

2 teaspoons salt

4 medium potatoes, peeled and very thinly sliced (prepped weight 1 lb 2 oz/500g)

For the salmon sauce

3 tablespoons olive oil

1 large cinnamon stick

2 bay leaves

1 onion, diced

5 large cloves of garlic, minced

½ teaspoon salt

1 tablespoon tomato paste

1 tablespoon chile flakes

1 x 14-oz/400g can of cream of tomato soup

10½ oz/300g raw salmon fillets

¾ oz/20g chives, chopped

For the bechamel sauce

7 tablespoons/100g unsalted butter

¾ cup/100g all-purpose flour

2½ cups/600ml whole milk

½ teaspoon salt

1¾ oz/50g mature cheddar cheese, grated

Before the purists start on at me, I should say I love moussaka with ground meat of any variety, but this is a really yummy alternative and a riff on something that already works. Because I have teenagers-slash-growing-men to feed, I often need to vary things up, so I love cooking this version with its layers of thin potatoes, eggplant, salmon scented with cinnamon in a rich tomato sauce, and a thick creamy bechamel. Hate me all you like, but you will love this!

Preheat the oven to 400°F and have a large baking sheet at the ready.

Start by prepping the eggplant. Once the stalks are removed and the eggplant sliced into ½-inch/1cm-thick pieces, add the oil to the baking sheet and pop the eggplant in. Get your hands in and get the eggplant all covered in a small amount of oil. Sprinkle with the salt and pop into the oven to roast for 30 minutes.

Start on the salmon sauce by adding the oil to a pan with the cinnamon and bay and allowing them to sizzle in the oil on medium heat for a few seconds. Add the diced onion and cook on high heat till the onion is golden and translucent, then add the minced garlic and cook for 5 minutes.

Add the salt, tomato paste, and chile flakes. Pour in the tomato soup and let everything just simmer away for a few minutes while you prep the salmon.

If your salmon has the skin still on, pop it into a dish or high-sided plate, skin-side up. Pour hot water over the skin. Let rest for 1 minute and you should very easily be able to just peel off the skin.

Take the fillets and pop into the pan with the tomato soup mix. Stir and put the lid on, then cook on medium heat for 5 minutes. Take the lid off and, using a spoon, break the fish up into flakes. Cook on medium to high heat till the fish is cooked through and the sauce has reduced a little.

By now the eggplant should be done, softened, and have taken on some color. Take out, set aside, and lower the oven temperature to 350°F. Take the salmon pan off the heat and add most of the chives, saving just a small handful for later.

Now to start layering. Take a 9 x 13-inch/23 x 33cm roasting dish. Layer half of the potatoes into the base. Add half the cooked eggplant on top, making sure to push it all down so you have an even layer. Now, pour in the fish mixture, making sure to remove the cinnamon and bay as you spoon it out. Spread into an even layer.

Add the remainder of the potato slices in a thin layer over the salmon, then add the rest of the eggplant in a thin layer.

Now, on to the bechamel sauce. Put the butter in a small pan and whisk on medium heat till melted. Add the flour and continue to mix till you have a smooth roux mixture that looks like it's coming away from the side of the pan.

Add a third of the milk and continue to whisk. As soon as it has thickened, add another third of the milk and when the mixture has thickened again, add the rest of the milk and keep whisking for 3 minutes, till you have a thick, rich, creamy bechamel sauce. Season with salt and pour all over the eggplant, evening out into a smooth layer. Add the grated cheese on top and sprinkle with the remaining chives.

Bake for 40–45 minutes. The moussaka should be bubbling and golden and make the kitchen smell incredible.

I would give it 30 minutes before eating—it's too hot otherwise. This time will allow the layers to settle, and you will appreciate the flavors so much more without burning the roof of your mouth. You know the rebel in you wants to give it a try. But don't!

anchovy crumb pasta

Serves 4

For the anchovy crumb

7 oz/200g white bread, cut into cubes

2 tablespoons olive oil

6 anchovy fillets

For the pasta

1 lb 2 oz/500g linguine

½ cup plus 2 tablespoons/150g unsalted butter

6 cloves of garlic, minced

2 anchovy fillets

3 onions, thinly sliced

handful of chopped fresh flat-leaf parsley

1 lemon, finely grated zest and juice

This is rich, salty, creamy, and heart-warming. The oven-baked salty anchovy breadcrumbs can be used to top literally anything. Here I've added them to simple onions and garlic cooked in rich butter and mixed with linguine, the pasta of choice in our home.

Start by preheating the oven to 400°F.

Place the cubed bread pieces on a large baking sheet, drizzle with the olive oil, and pop into the oven to bake for 20 minutes.

Cook the linguine as per the instructions on the package, making sure to season the water well. This can take up to 9 minutes.

Add the butter to a large pan and heat till it's just brown, then turn down the heat and add the garlic and the 2 anchovy fillets. As soon as the garlic is golden, add the onion and cook till just caramelized and softened. This could take 10 minutes.

Drain the pasta, reserving a little of the starchy water. Add the drained pasta to the onion and mix well, along with a ladleful of the pasta cooking water, mixing till the water has evaporated.

Take the toasted bread pieces out of the oven and pop into a food processor with the anchovies. Blitz to create a golden, salty crumb.

Add 2 tablespoons of the crumb mixture to the pasta, then add a handful of chopped parsley and the zest and juice of the lemon and mix well. Serve up a portion, sprinkle with a generous amount of the anchovy crumb, and you are ready to eat.

baked apple fritters with lime and raspberry icing

Serves 15	Vegetarian

1 large green apple, peeled, cored, and diced into ¼-inch/ 5mm cubes (5¼ oz/150g)

packed ½ cup/110g brown sugar

½ cup plus 2 tablespoons/150g unsalted butter, melted, plus extra for greasing

1 large egg

1 teaspoon vanilla bean paste

1¾ cups plus 1 tablespoon/230g all-purpose flour

2½ teaspoons baking powder

½ teaspoon salt

½ cup/9g freeze-dried raspberries

For the icing

2 cups/250g confectioners' sugar, sifted

1 lime, finely grated zest and 1 tablespoon juice

3 tablespoons water

5 raspberries

As much as I love deep-frying, it's good to have an alternative. Any time I have ordered fritters from a restaurant menu, the apple is rock solid, the batter tastes like potato, and they're covered in a syrup, so I always find them just not very nice. I'm sure there are many places that make delicious fritters; please point me in their direction. Till then we have these ones, with soft baked apples and raspberries, covered in a sweet lime and raspberry icing.

Start by prepping the apple, a job worth doing slowly and nibbling along the way. Once the apple has been diced, set it aside.

Preheat the oven to 400°F and have three baking sheets ready, lightly greased with butter and lined with parchment paper.

Combine the brown sugar and butter in a bowl and mix well. Now add the egg and vanilla paste and mix again. Throw in the flour, baking powder, salt, and freeze-dried raspberries and mix well till you have something that looks like a really thick cake batter, almost like cookie dough. Add the apple cubes and mix till well combined.

Take 2 tablespoons of the mix and place on a prepared baking sheet in a mound. Repeat, making sure you allow space between the mounds as they will spread a little. Pop six mounds on two sheets and three on the third sheet.

Bake for about 10 minutes, till they have spread a little and are golden brown around the edges. Take them out and allow to cool completely on the sheet. This will help them to hold their shape. Once cool, transfer them one by one to a cooling rack. Set paper under the rack to catch any drips of icing.

Make the icing by combining the confectioners' sugar, lime zest, juice, and water in a bowl with the raspberries. Mix to crush the raspberries and bring the icing together. Pour spoonfuls of the icing over the fritters, making sure to cover each and allowing it to drip down the sides. Allow the icing to just set a little and then they are ready to eat.

toasted sweet brioche with orange, saffron, cardamom, and pistachio

| Serves 4 | Vegetarian |

This is like an instant bread-and-butter pudding dish, with all the flavors of Indian sweets but less of the sugar. Simply spiced and topped off with crème fraîche and pistachios, it's warm, sweet, and fragrant, and ready in minutes.

Preheat the oven to 350°F and have a baking sheet at the ready.

Pop the four thick slices of brioche onto the sheet. Brush the soft ghee on both sides of each slice and bake in the oven for 10 minutes.

Meanwhile, make the syrup by combining the sugar and orange zest in a small pan. Add the juice of the orange to a liquid measuring cup and top it up with enough water to get you to 1 cup/240ml of liquid. Pour into the pan with the sugar. Add the pinch of saffron.

4 x 1-inch/2.5cm-thick slices store-bought brioche

¼ cup/50g ghee (clarified butter), melted

For the syrup

¾ cup/150g sugar

1 orange, finely grated zest and juice, plus extra water to make up to 1 cup/240ml

a pinch of saffron

6 cardamom pods, crushed

To finish

whipped cream

1 orange, finely grated zest only

¼ cup/30g shelled pistachios, chopped

Use a mortar and pestle to remove the husk from the cardamom pods and grind the tiny black seeds to a fine powder. Add to the syrup pan. Mix well and then bring to a boil. As soon as it comes to a boil, lower to medium heat and simmer for 10 minutes, till the mixture has just thickened slightly.

Once the brioche has had 10 minutes, turn all four slices over and bake for 5 minutes. Once golden all over, take out and drizzle the hot syrup over the brioche and allow the mixture to soak in it for a few minutes.

To serve, take a piece of brioche, add a large dollop of crème fraîche, zest over some orange, sprinkle with the pistachios, and it is ready to devour.

hot chocolate custard cake

Serves 8–10   Vegetarian

1 cup/125g all-purpose flour

½ cup plus 2 tablespoons/120g sugar

1 teaspoon baking powder

¼ cup/20g cocoa powder

¼ teaspoon salt

½ cup/120ml whole milk

1 large egg

6 tablespoons/80g unsalted butter, melted, plus extra for greasing

For the sauce

1 cup/240ml boiling water

¼ cup/20g cocoa powder

¾ cup/150g sugar

1 tablespoon instant coffee

2 tablespoons coffee creamer

This is every chocolate lover's dream. It's magical not just because it's delicious but also because of what happens in the oven. A simple sweet cocoa cake batter is topped with a hot chocolate liquid that magically turns into custard when baked! It's hot, it's warming, and it's quick. Perfect for a midweek chocolate fix.

Preheat the oven to 350°F. Have a greased 9-inch/23cm square baking pan ready.

Start by making the cake. Add the flour, sugar, baking powder, cocoa, and salt straight into the pan and whisk to combine. Add the milk, egg, and butter and mix till you have a smooth cake batter. Spread with the back of a spoon into an even layer.

Make the sauce by pouring the boiling water into a liquid measuring cup. Now, add the cocoa powder, sugar, coffee, and creamer and whisk to combine. You may find it's a little bit lumpy, but that's okay, don't worry. The magic will still happen, I promise.

Take a spoon, turn it curved-side up over the baking pan and pour the chocolate liquid directly onto the spoon—this will prevent the pouring liquid from creating a massive great big hole in the cake batter as it's being poured. Once you have poured on all of the liquid, pop the dish into the oven.

Bake for 25 minutes and, as if by magic, there will be a custard layer on the bottom and a cake layer on the top. You should see the custard bubbling around the edge.

Take the cake out of the oven and let rest for 5 minutes. This will allow the custard to just thicken slightly and for the whole thing to cool a little or you will burn the roof of your mouth—and you will need your mouth to taste this beauty!

Spoon the cake and the sauce into bowls. I like to serve this with a good old store-bought raspberry ripple ice cream.

white chocolate and raspberry puff bar

Serves 4–6	**Vegetarian**

flour, for dusting

1 lb 2 oz/500g frozen puff pastry, defrosted

3½ oz/100g white chocolate bar

3 tablespoons semolina

1¼ cups/150g dried apricots, chopped

1¼ cups/ 150g fresh raspberries

⅓ cup/50g pistachios, roughly chopped

1 egg, beaten

2 tablespoons marmalade

This epic puff bar is made with store-bought puff pastry and filled with layers of chewy apricot, white chocolate, raspberries, and pistachios, for a thing of beauty and simplicity!

Lightly flour a work surface and roll out the puff pastry to a 10 x 14-inch/25 x 35cm rectangle. Put the pastry on a sheet of parchment paper and place onto a baking sheet—this is easiest to do now, before you start loading it up.

Orient the pastry in front of you with one of the short sides closest to you. Place the bar of chocolate in the center, vertically, and use a knife to mark around the bar. Remove the bar and set aside.

Fill the marked rectangle with the semolina, spread to an even layer. Place the dried apricots on top of the semolina, inside the marked rectangle. Now add the whole bar of white chocolate right on top. Arrange a layer of the raspberries on top of the chocolate, then sprinkle the pistachios over the raspberries and into the gaps.

You can refer to the photos on the next page to help with the next stage. Use a sharp knife to cut diagonally from one top corner of the pastry all the way to the nearest corner of the fillings. Do the same for all four corners. Brush the cuts with the beaten egg.

Lift the top flap, the one furthest away from you, and fold it up so it encloses the chocolate bar and fillings. Lightly press the pastry to the fillings so it stays upright. Do the same with the pastry flap closest to you, pressing it onto the side of the chocolate and fillings. Now take the long edge on the right and bring it up to encase the filling. Use a little beaten egg to stick the pastry to the short ends you have just secured and press to seal. Repeat with the other long side. You should end up with the chocolate and fillings neatly tucked into a pastry boat. If the pastry comes up higher than the fillings, neatly trim off the excess pastry with a sharp knife. Brush all over with egg wash and chill in the fridge for 30 minutes.

Preheat the oven to 400°F and put a baking sheet in the oven to start getting it really hot.

Take the pastry out of the fridge, brush again with beaten egg and use the parchment paper to lift it onto the preheated sheet. Bake for 40–45 minutes, till light golden and puffy.

Take the marmalade and warm it till runny, then use it to brush all over the pastry to create a beautiful glossy sheen. Let cool for just 30 minutes and cut into slices to eat.

I love this served with sweet, cool mascarpone cream.

→

chapter two
CHILL-OUT DAYS

sweet onion socca

For the batter

1⅓ cups/125g chickpea flour (gram flour), sifted

2 teaspoons onion seeds

2 tablespoons onion granules

1 tablespoon garlic granules

½ teaspoon salt

1¼ cups/290ml cold water

For the onions

¼ cup/50g unsalted butter, melted

a large sprig of fresh thyme

3 onions, thinly sliced

1 teaspoon salt

1 teaspoon sugar

To serve

2½ oz/75g Gruyère cheese, grated (⅔ cup)

fresh chives, finely chopped

Serves 2   Vegetarian/Gluten-free

Socca is an Italian/French pancake made from chickpea flour, an ingredient that is commonly used in many Southeast Asian homes. It's funny how just one ingredient can make something feel so familiar. Here I am taking some influence from a French onion soup and making a deliciously sweet breakfast socca of caramelized sweet onions with a hint of thyme and melting Gruyère.

Start by making the batter. Add the sifted flour to a bowl. (It's important to sift the flour because chickpea flour has more moisture than all-purpose flour, so it clumps easily. So, while sifting you will find it doesn't billow through like other flours. Use the back of a spoon to encourage it through.)

To the flour, add the onion seeds, onion and garlic granules, and salt, and whisk to combine. Make a well in the center, add the cold water, and whisk till you have a smooth batter. Cover with a clean kitchen towel and let rest for 30 minutes.

Preheat the oven to 400°F.

Add the butter to an 8½-inch/22cm (bottom measurement) oven-safe frying pan along with the sprig of thyme and sliced onion and pop into the oven for 10 minutes. Take out, stir, add the salt and sugar, and pop back in for another 10 minutes.

Take out and stir again. Remove the sprig of thyme, making sure to pull off any of the cooked leaves and add them back in with the onion. Discard the twiggy bit. Mix the onion and spread out evenly across the pan.

Now, take the chickpea batter mixture and give it a stir to mix in all the onion seeds again as they will have risen to the top. Pour carefully in and around the onion till you have an even layer. Pop into the oven and bake for 10–12 minutes, till the batter mix looks dry on top and not shiny as it was when it first went in.

Take out, turn on the broiler to high, sprinkle with the cheese, and broil till the cheese has melted and is bubbling. This will take less than 1 minute. Set aside for 5 minutes to cool a little. Sprinkle with a good amount of chives and you are ready to slice and eat.

sprinkle butter babka loaf

Serves 8–10	Vegetarian

For the dough

2¼ cups/275g all-purpose flour, plus extra for dusting

1¾ teaspoons fast-acting dried yeast

2 tablespoons sugar

¼ teaspoon salt

2 large eggs, beaten

3 tablespoons whole milk

6 tablespoons/80g unsalted butter, softened, plus extra for greasing

For the filling

7 tablespoons/100g unsalted butter, softened

½ cup/100g sugar

¾ cup/140g rainbow sprinkles, plus 2 tablespoons extra for the top

For the syrup

3 tablespoons golden syrup or light corn syrup

1 tablespoon hot water

It's traditional in Holland to have a slice of white bread buttered and sprinkled—and when I say sprinkled, I mean doused in chocolate sprinkles. Take me to Holland! They had me at bread and butter, let alone sprinkles. So, this is my all-in-one version: a rolled babka bread dough with colored sprinkles swirled through, then braided and baked. Based on a traditional Jewish sweet bread, it pleases not only the baker in me, but also the eight-year-old in me!

Start by lightly greasing and lining the inside of a 9 x 5-inch/900g loaf pan.

Now, let's make the dough by placing the flour in the bowl of a stand mixer or in a large bowl if you are making it by hand. Add the yeast and sugar to one side of the flour and the salt to the other.

Give it a quick mix and make a well in the center. Add the beaten eggs and the milk and mix till the dough starts to come together. If you're using a stand mixer, attach a dough hook and start to bring the dough together.

Slowly start adding the butter in clumps till fully incorporated. Knead on high speed for 6 minutes. If you are kneading by hand, use as little flour as possible and knead for about 10 minutes till the dough is smooth and shiny and stretchy. Lightly flour the work surface and roll out the dough to a rectangle of 8 x 12 inches/20 x 30cm.

Make the sprinkle butter by mixing the soft butter with the sugar and half the sprinkles.

Orient the dough rectangle with one of the long edges closest to you. Spread the sprinkle butter all over the rectangle, leaving an edge of ½-inch/1cm all the way around. Take the rest of the sprinkles and spread all over evenly and push into the dough.

Now, roll up the dough like a cinnamon bun, starting at the long edge. Make sure to roll tight. Lift the roll and place it in front of you vertically, seam-side down. Using a sharp knife, start at the top of the roll and cut it in half vertically all the way down, all the way through. So now you should have two long pieces of dough. Turn them out so you can see stripes of dough and sprinkle butter.

→

Make a large cross using the two dough strips. Crisscross the whole thing like a two-strand braid till you reach the end. Gently lift and pop into the prepared pan, making sure to tuck under the ends. Cover with a piece of greased plastic wrap and let rise in a warm place till doubled in size.

Preheat the oven to 400°F.

Bake the loaf in the oven for 15 minutes. Lower the heat to 350°F and then continue to bake for 20–25 minutes, making sure the top of the loaf doesn't get too dark. Take out and let cool for 15 minutes before removing from the pan.

Make the syrup glaze by mixing the golden syrup and water. Brush the loaf all over with the sticky glaze and scatter with the extra sprinkles.

Once the loaf has cooled down, slice and it's ready to eat. Nobody is stopping you from adding more butter and sprinkles, if you so wish, in fact I highly recommend it!

surprise snickerdoodles

Serves 20   Vegetarian

20 small chocolate caramel cups (approx. 2½ packages)

5 tablespoons/75g unsalted butter, plus extra for greasing

7 oz/200g dark chocolate, chopped

packed ½ cup/100g brown sugar

3 large eggs

1 teaspoon vanilla extract

½ teaspoon almond extract

2¾ cups/350g all-purpose flour

1 teaspoon baking powder

For the coating

1 cup/150g salted peanuts, finely chopped or blitzed

½ teaspoon ground cinnamon

A snickerdoodle is a sweet American cookie that's traditionally coated in cinnamon. This is exactly that but taken to the next level with a bit of chocolate, the delicious nuttiness of salted peanuts, and a gooey caramel surprise inside.

Pop the chocolate caramel cups onto a plate and chill in the freezer.

To make the dough, combine the butter and chocolate in a pot and melt till you have a mixture that is viscous. Take off the heat, pour into a large bowl, add the brown sugar, and mix. Now let cool for 10 minutes.

Add the eggs, vanilla, almond, flour, and baking powder and mix everything till you have a dough that is stiff and easy to handle. Divide the mixture into 20 equal mounds. Take the chocolates out of the freezer.

Take each dough mound and flatten. Pop a frozen caramel choc in the center and fold the cookie dough over to encase the chocolate. Roll into a ball and pop onto a baking sheet. Do this to all 20.

Now, mix the peanuts with the cinnamon really well.

Roll each dough ball in the peanut mixture, pressing and pushing the peanut mix into the dough. Do this to all 20. Just push them down a tiny bit to gently flatten the top. Put on a plate and chill in the fridge for 1 hour or in the freezer for 30 minutes.

Preheat the oven to 400°F and lightly grease and line two baking sheets.

Transfer the chilled dough balls to the prepared sheets about 2 inches/5cm apart so they have room to spread. Bake for 13 minutes.

Take them out and allow them to cool completely on the sheets before eating. Break in half and enjoy a cocoa snickerdoodle with its caramel surprise inside!

tandoori chicken naan sando

Serves 2

For the cabbage slaw
3½ oz/100g red cabbage, finely shredded (about ⅛ of a cabbage)

3½ oz/100g green onions, finely sliced

1 green apple, grated

1 lemon, finely grated zest and juice

a pinch of salt

For the chicken
oil, for greasing

2 chicken breasts (1 lb 2 oz/500g)

3 tablespoons tandoori paste

1 tablespoon chickpea flour (gram flour)

½ teaspoon cayenne pepper

a pinch of salt

For the sauce
4 heaped tablespoons mayonnaise

1 clove of garlic, minced

a small handful of fresh mint leaves

a small handful of fresh cilantro

To serve
3 plain mini naans (9 oz/250g)

3 store-bought poppadoms

I have seen these sandos knocking around everywhere. It's essentially breaded protein (usually pork) that is deep-fried and beautifully sandwiched between neat toasted white bread. Aesthetically pleasing, yes, but I wanted to make my own version of an epic sando crossed with an Indian sandwich. So, mine has fragrant tandoori chicken in between layers of soft naan, with minty mayo, crisp cabbage and—the best bit—crunchy poppadoms! Beautifully brilliant and mouth-wateringly delicious.

Start with the slaw because it will need the most time to macerate and soften. Put the shredded red cabbage in a bowl along with the green onion, grated apple, lemon zest, juice, and salt. Get your hands in and really squeeze the mixture together. Set aside and allow it to soften in the juices.

Now, on to the chicken. Preheat the oven to 425°F. Have a greased roasting dish ready.

Next, you need to butterfly the chicken breasts. You do this by laying a breast piece vertically with the tapered end closest to you. Place a hand on top of the chicken and, using a sharp knife and starting at the top, thicker end, start cutting into the breast along the side and down to the tapered end. Be sure not to cut all the way through. Now, open it like a book and you should have a kind of heart shape. Flatten using your hand. Repeat with the other breast.

In a small bowl, mix the tandoori paste, chickpea flour, cayenne, and salt. I like to get in there with my hands. Spread a thin layer over one side of each butterflied chicken breast. Lay the chicken paste-side down in the dish and smother the rest of the paste generously over the top of the chicken breasts. Bake in the oven for 25 minutes.

→

Meanwhile, make the sauce by combining the mayo, garlic, mint leaves, and cilantro in a bowl and mixing really well.

Once the chicken is cooked, take it out and remove it from any cooking juices. While the oven is hot, put the naans into the oven to warm slightly. Take out after 3 minutes and turn the oven off.

Now, continue with the slaw. You will see that it is sitting in a lot of juices that we don't want in our sando. Put the cabbage mix in the center of a clean kitchen towel, bring the edge to the center and squeeze any juices right out.

Time to start building the layers of our gorgeous sando sarnie. Start with a sheet of parchment paper large enough to wrap this thing. Place a warm naan in the center and smother on some of that minted mayo. Now, take slabs of your chicken and pile it on, making sure the chicken stays within the parameters of your naan. Where it doesn't, cut it off and place the offcut somewhere else in the sandwich. Do this till you've used up all your chicken. This is going to be monumental, as all good sandwiches should be!

Add another piece of naan right on top. Smother with the mayo and pile on the cabbage slaw. Take the poppadoms and add straight on top again, breaking where you need to, to fit it all in. Add the last naan on top.

This is the best bit—press down firmly to get all those layers really stuck together. Use the paper to wrap the whole sandwich nice and tight, like a big sweetie. Cut down the middle, through the paper and you will have two epic, gargantuan tandoori sandos!

baked chicken curry stew

Serves 4–6
Gluten-free

For the sauce

½ cup plus
2 tablespoons/150g
clarified butter
(ghee)

3 tablespoons garam
masala

2 onions, roughly
chopped

2 red bell peppers,
roughly chopped

1 teaspoon ground
turmeric

4 tablespoons garlic
and ginger paste

1 teaspoon chile
powder

1 tablespoon salt

8 boneless, skinless
chicken thighs

2 large potatoes,
peeled (14 oz/400g)

2 tablespoons mango
pickle

1 cup/240ml water

To serve

a large handful of
fresh cilantro

chopped red chiles

lemon wedges

cooked basmati rice

All good curries need time and patience and just a little bit of attention. Sounds like I'm writing about the key to a successful marriage, but no, this is also key to a pretty yummy curry. This delicious chicken curry is cooked gently, like a stew, and because it's nearly entirely done in the oven, you won't break a bead of sweat in the process. Traditional, no, but baking it means you can chill out while still ending up with something aromatic and delicious.

Preheat the oven to 400°F.

Add the clarified butter to a large Dutch oven (with a lid), pop onto high heat, and allow the butter to melt. Turn the heat down and add the garam masala.

Now, place the onion and bell pepper in a blender with a splash of water and blitz to a smooth paste. Add this directly to the Dutch oven and cook on high heat till the paste is just golden. Take off the heat.

Add the turmeric, garlic and ginger paste, chile, and salt and mix well. Add the chicken thigh pieces, whole, along with the two whole potatoes and the mango pickle. Give everything a good mix. Add the water and mix again.

Pop into the oven with the lid on and cook for 2 hours. After 1 hour, the chicken should just fall apart and the potato should be tender. The sole purpose of the potato is to thicken the sauce, so move the chicken to one side of the pan (but still in the pan) and use a potato masher to really mash that potato, which will help you thicken the sauce without adding any flour. Once mashed, give it all a mix.

Take electric beaters—the kind you would use to whip egg whites or make a cake, except this time we're using it to shred chicken. Gently move the beaters in the pot and you will see your chicken shred effortlessly.

Serve the curry hot, sprinkled with the cilantro and red chiles, along with a wedge of lemon and a side of rice.

smashed spiced chickpeas

7 tablespoons/100ml olive oil

1 large egg white

2 x 15-oz/425g cans of chickpeas, drained

1½ tablespoons cornstarch

1 teaspoon salt

1 lemon, finely grated zest only

¼ cup/25g za'atar

1 tablespoon sumac

Serves 4 (as a snack)	Gluten-free

Chickpeas were a staple in my home long before they became trendy or even popular. Whether canned, dried, boiled, in flour form, or as a snack, my family and I have been eating them forever and a day. As a kid, I didn't much appreciate them, but my goodness I love chickpeas now and I could eat them by the bucket load. When turned into this crunchy snack they are mind-blowing, packed with flavor from the za'atar and sumac, and so simple to make.

Start by preheating the oven to 400°F. Grab a rimmed baking sheet and drizzle the oil into the sheet, making sure it has spread all over. Put the sheet into the oven to really get that oil hot.

In the meantime, add the egg white to a bowl and whisk till frothy.

Make sure the chickpeas are as dry as possible—give them a quick wipe with paper towels. This will help them crisp up better. Throw them into the egg whites and mix till they are covered in the whites.

In a small bowl, mix the cornstarch, salt, lemon zest, za'atar, and sumac.

Take the sheet of hot oil out of the oven. Add the spices to the chickpeas and mix thoroughly till everything is covered. Spread the mixture carefully into the sheet on the hot oil, in one even layer. Bake for 15 minutes.

Take out of the oven. Using the bottom of a glass or tumbler, squash the chickpeas so they break and flatten—these ridges, once baked, will create a whole lot of texture.

Bake for 12–15 minutes, till crisp. Give the chickpeas a good shake or stir to break them up. Return them to the oven for 5-minute bursts if they still need some more crisping up.

Take out and let cool completely on the sheet and they are ready to adorn that snack table.

green onion pancakes

3¼ cups/400g all-purpose flour, plus extra for dusting

1 teaspoon salt

2 tablespoons vegetable oil, plus extra oil for brushing

¾ cup plus 2 tablespoons/ 200ml cold water

For the filling

¼ cup/60g garlic and ginger paste

9 oz/250g green onions, thinly sliced, just the green parts

chile oil, for brushing

To serve

kimchi

yogurt

frilly fried eggs

Serves 6   Vegetarian

These are pancakes-slash-parathas-slash-roti-slash-delicious! A simple pastry recipe, filled and rolled with garlic, ginger, and loads of green onion, they are subtle and sweet with a great onion hit. Hot out of the oven and smothered in chile oil, they're perfect for a weekend lunch.

Start by adding the flour to a large bowl with the salt and drizzling in the oil. Using a spatula or butter knife, mix the ingredients together.

Make a well in the center and add the water. Mix with the knife till all the water has disappeared. Cover your hands in oil—just rub some oil into the palm of your hands—and bring the dough together. Don't be tempted to knead. Bring it together with the palms of your hands and with your knuckles, till you have a dough that has come together and is smooth.

The bowl should be totally clean of any flour. Cover with a clean kitchen towel and let rest for 15–20 minutes, or longer if you are busy.

Preheat the oven to 400°F. Brush two large baking sheets with oil.

Flour a work surface lightly and divide the mixture into six mounds, approx. 3½ oz/105g each. Roll out each piece of dough to an 8½-inch/22cm square. Take a small spoonful of the garlic and ginger paste and spread it all over each square in an even layer. Sprinkle with a generous amount of the green onion.

Now, roll up the dough like you would a cinnamon bun, till you reach the end, then roll up into a coil, so you have what looks like the swirl of a snail's shell. Tuck the last bit underneath.

Dust the surface again if you need to and use a rolling pin to roll out the coil into a flattened circle of 4 inches/10cm. It will still be quite thick, but that is perfect. Pop on an oiled baking sheet. Carry on doing the same till you have finished all six.

Brush the tops with a little oil. Cover with foil and bake for 10 minutes. Take out and flip over, cover again with the foil, and bake for another 10 minutes. They should be just lightly golden brown.

Once they are fully baked, let cool on the sheet till they are not too hot to handle. Brush with some chile oil. These are delicious with a side of kimchi and yogurt and topped with a frilly fried egg. Or even simply with a side salad. A scrummy, perfect lunch!

baked shrimp pasta dinner

Serves 6–8

1 lb 2 oz/500g dried pasta (conchigliette)

2½ quarts/2.5 liters boiling water

a large pinch of salt

7 tablespoons/100g salted butter

4 large cloves of garlic, minced

10½ oz/300g cherry tomatoes, halved

10 anchovy fillets

2 tablespoons tomato paste

2 teaspoons chilli flakes

2 tablespoons balsamic vinegar

2 cups/500g uncooked tomato purée

1 lb 1 oz/480g raw shrimp

5¼ oz/150g small fresh mozzarella balls, drained

To serve

fresh basil leaves

ground black pepper

balsamic vinegar

This is an all-in-one of everything we like in a dinner: easy, delicious, and not much standing over a pot, if at all, in fact. With the pasta pre-cooked; sauce made in the oven with sweet tomatoes and garlic; shrimp popped on top and all finished off in the oven, it's perfect for not overthinking dinner and just enjoying it with minimum effort.

Pour the pasta into a large pan, big enough to allow the pasta to expand. Pour in the boiling water, add a generous amount of salt, and give everything a really good stir. We are going to allow this to rest for 15 minutes to precook. Give it a stir occasionally.

Preheat the oven to 425°F.

Take a large roasting dish or deep casserole dish. To the dish add the butter, minced garlic, tomatoes, and anchovies and pop into the oven for 15 minutes.

Drain the pasta, reserving 1 cup/240ml of the starchy liquid.

Take the roasting dish out of the oven, squash down the cooked tomatoes, and break down the anchovies with the back of a spoon. Add the tomato paste, chile, balsamic, and tomato purée and mix really well.

Now, pour in the starchy water along with the pasta and mix well. Cover with foil and bake in the oven for 15 minutes. After 15 minutes, take the dish out of the oven, add the shrimp, and stir them in. Dot the mozzarella around and pop back in the oven, uncovered, for 10 minutes.

Take out of the oven and let rest for 10 minutes before serving to allow some of the liquid to absorb and for the food to cool slightly. Throw some basil leaves on top, sprinkle with some black pepper, and add one last drizzle of balsamic. Enjoy!

slow-cooked lamb daleem

Serves 6–8   Gluten-free

2¼ cups/200g rolled oats
¾ cup plus 2 tablespoons/ 200ml olive oil
2 large cinnamon sticks
3 bay leaves
1 tablespoon cumin seeds
3 large onions, finely diced
2 tablespoons salt

¾ cup plus 1 tablespoon/190g chopped garlic
¾ cup/180g chopped ginger
2 tablespoons garam masala
½ teaspoon ground turmeric 1 tablespoon chile powder
2 tablespoons ground coriander

1 x 15-oz/425g can of green lentils, drained
2 lb 2 oz/1kg lamb, diced
6⅓ cups/1.5 liters water

To serve
fresh ginger, cut into thin sticks
chopped green chiles
lemon wedges

Daleem is a slow-cooked hearty stew with everything that you can think of that is good for you. It's filling and it's warming—it's quite literally a hug in a bowl. I remember eating it during monsoon season in Bangladesh. I was traveling with my uncle back from my aunt's, which was a boat trip, a bus ride, and a 4-mile walk away. We got caught out in the rain and I'm so glad we did, as we sheltered in a badly lantern-lit stall that sold just one thing: daleem! A massive vat was surrounded by customers, all taking away dried banana leaf plates filled generously to the brim and served with soft bread. It's a taste memory that will stay with me for ever. So, I have created my own version for us to enjoy. We may not get monsoons, but we know a thing or two about miserable weather.

Preheat the oven to 400°F.

Pop a large frying pan onto high heat and add the oats straight in. Stir the oats till they are a lovely golden brown. Remove the pan from the heat and set aside.

Take a large Dutch oven, one that has a lid, and put on medium heat. Add the oil and as soon as it is hot, add the cinnamon, bay, and cumin seeds. As soon as the spices start to sizzle and you can smell them, add the onion and salt and mix till the onion has just a tiny bit of color.

Now add the garlic, ginger, garam masala, turmeric, chile, ground coriander, lentils, and lamb. Mix it all together and top off with the water. Add the toasted oats, which will really thicken the sauce and give a toasted flavor. Pop the lid on and bake for 2 hours. Check the curry, give it a good stir, and add a little more water, if necessary. Return to the oven for 1 hour.

Have all your serving bits ready: ginger sliced, chiles chopped, and wedges of lemon. Take the daleem out of the oven. It should be cooked till totally broken down. Some people like to blend this mixture, but I much prefer it to stay exactly as it is, with lots of texture.

Serve yourself a bowl. Sprinkle with the ginger, chile, and a good squeeze of lemon. You can even serve it with soft pillowy bread like I first had it.

charred tomato stromboli

For the dough

3½ cups/450g white bread flour, plus a little extra for dusting

⅓ cup/50g semolina

4 teaspoons black sesame seeds

1 x ¼-oz/7g packet of fast-acting dried yeast

1 teaspoon salt

2 tablespoons olive oil

1⅓ cups/325ml warm water

grated parmesan cheese, to sprinkle

For the sauce

4 tomatoes

6 cloves of garlic

1 small onion, roughly chopped

1 teaspoon salt

1 teaspoon sugar

2 teaspoons dried oregano

3 tablespoons olive oil

For the filling

2½ oz/75g bacon or meat-free bacon (2–3 slices), finely chopped

4½ oz/125g shredded mozzarella (mounded 1 cup)

a large handful of fresh basil leaves

To serve

olive oil

a drizzle of balsamic vinegar

This is such a simple recipe, like pizza in a savory cinnamon bun form. What I love most about it is the smoky-sweet flavor of the charred tomato, which is really enhanced by the garlic. It works so well with the bacon and creamy cheese all wrapped up in a soft dough.

Start by making the dough. Place the flour in a bowl with the semolina and sesame seeds. Give it a good mix. Add the yeast to one side of the bowl and the salt to the other and mix again. Drizzle in the oil and mix well. Make a well in the center, add the water, and mix using a rubber spatula.

Begin kneading, either by hand or using a stand mixer with a dough hook attached. If you are using a mixer, knead for 6 minutes on high speed. If you are doing it by hand, knead on a lightly floured surface for about 12 minutes or at least till the dough is smooth, stretchy, and elastic. Pop into a lightly greased bowl, cover with plastic wrap, and let rise in a warm spot till doubled in size.

Now, get on to the sauce. You will need three metal skewers. Skewer your tomatoes, two on each skewer, and then all the garlic on the third skewer.

Turn your gas stove on to high heat and carefully pass all your tomatoes across the flame till completely black and charred. Set aside and do the same to the garlic. Add the charred tomatoes and garlic to a food processor. Now add the onion, salt, sugar, and oregano and blitz to a smooth paste.

Heat the oil in a small pot, add the tomato mixture, and cook on medium heat till all the water has evaporated and you have a rich, thick, dark tomato sauce. This can take up to 15 minutes. Let cool completely.

Lightly flour the work surface, uncover your dough, and tip out. Roll out the dough to a rectangle, 16 x 12 inches/ 40 x 30cm. With the long side of the rectangle closest to you, spread the cooled tomato mixture all over the dough, leaving a bare edge all the way around. Sprinkle with the sliced bacon and then the grated mozzarella. Tear up the basil and sprinkle it all over the mozzarella.

Have a lightly greased baking sheet at the ready. Start rolling the dough from the edge closest to you, like a cinnamon bun. Pinch the ends to seal in the filling. Gently lift the rolled-up dough and place onto the sheet. Cover with greased plastic wrap and let rise in a warm place for 30 minutes.

Preheat the oven to 400°F. Sprinkle some grated parmesan over the rolled-up dough and then bake for 25 minutes. As soon as it is done, let cool for 30 minutes. Slice and serve with olive oil mixed with a drizzle of balsamic. Yum!

butterscotch cheesecake coconut bars

Serves 10   Vegetarian

1 lb 2 oz/500g frozen puff pastry, defrosted

7 oz/200g speculoos cookies

½ cup/50g dried shredded coconut, toasted

5 tablespoons/75g salted butter, melted

For the filling

1 lb 5 oz/600g full-fat cream cheese

1 vanilla pod

¼ cup/50g sugar

1 large egg, beaten

2 tablespoons all-purpose flour

3½ oz/100g soft caramels, chopped

For the top

1 tablespoon unsalted butter, melted

2 tablespoons sugar

½ teaspoon nutmeg

½ teaspoon ground cinnamon

These bars are so yummy with their layers of buttery puff pastry (easy store-bought!), cookie coconut crumb and cheesecake filling dotted with soft caramels, all topped with even more of that crumb and pastry under a sweet crunchy top. All the flavors of butterscotch with its caramels and vanilla, plus a sweet hint of coconut and spice. Pure and utter joy!

Start by lining the bottom and sides of an 8-inch/20cm square cake pan. Preheat the oven to 375°F.

Cut the pastry in half. Take one rectangle of dough and squash it into a round ball—the aim is to still have a buttery dough but with fewer layers. Do this to both pieces. Now roll out the pastry into a rough square and trim to an 8-inch/20cm square to fit the cake pan. Do this to both mounds of pastry. Place one square of pastry in the bottom and keep the other one off to the side.

Put the cookies into a food processor and blitz to a fine crumb. Pour into a bowl with the toasted coconut and butter and mix well. Add half of the crumb mixture right on top of the pastry in the pan and push that into the pastry.

To make the filling, put the cream cheese into a bowl. Scrape out the seeds of the vanilla pod and add to the cream cheese along with the sugar, egg, and flour and mix well. Stir in the chopped caramels. Spread the mixture all over the cookie crumb.

Now add the remaining cookie crumb in another layer and then the second square of pastry on top. Push it down to create an even, flat layer.

Brush the top with melted butter. Mix the sugar with the nutmeg and cinnamon and sprinkle all over the top. Bake for 35–40 minutes.

Take out and let rest in the pan till completely cool. Chill for 2 hours and then, after all the waiting, it is ready to cut into bars and eat.

marbled ice cream loaf cake

Serves 6–8   Vegetarian

Made from very few ingredients, this cake's hero ingredient is defrosted ice cream. It is one of my absolute favorite cakes to make. Why? Because it's simple. Another reason? It's a way of adding more ice cream to my diet. It's so much fun, marbled with strawberry and chocolate. Way cool!

For the cake

oil, for greasing

1 cup/150g strawberry ice cream, defrosted completely

1 cup/150g chocolate ice cream, defrosted completely

1 cup plus 2 tablespoons/140g all-purpose flour, sifted

1½ teaspoons baking powder

¼ teaspoon salt

½ cup/9g freeze-dried strawberry pieces

For the topping

5¼ oz/150g dark chocolate, chopped

⅔ cup/160ml heavy cream

5¼ oz/150g strawberries, halved

Start by preheating the oven to 375°F. Line and lightly grease a 9 x 5-inch/900g loaf pan.

Put the defrosted ice creams in two separate bowls—what we want is two distinct colors that we can marble.

In a third bowl, mix together the flour, baking powder, and salt.

To the strawberry ice cream, add the freeze-dried strawberries and mix well. Add half of the flour mixture and stir till you have a batter. Do the same with the chocolate ice cream, adding the flour and mixing till you have a smooth batter.

Now, a spoonful at a time, alternate the batter into the prepared cake pan, till you have used up all of both mixtures. Take a long skewer and, using sweeping motions, gently marble the mixture. Pop into the oven to bake for 30–35 minutes.

While the cake bakes, make the ganache. Put the chopped chocolate in a bowl. Place the cream in a pan and put it on medium to high heat. As soon as the cream just starts to come up to a boil, but is not actually boiling, take it off the heat.

Pour the hot cream all over the chocolate and stir till you have no more chunks of chocolate and a rich, smooth, glossy mixture. Pop it into the fridge and let chill for 30 minutes.

Take the cake out of the oven and allow to cool in the pan for 10 minutes before removing and cooling completely on a rack.

Remove the ganache from the fridge—it should be cooled and smooth and easy to spoon, not completely hardened. Whisk the ganache mixture till light and fluffy and doubled in size. Pop into a piping bag with a star nozzle attached and pipe all over the top of the cake. Dress with halved strawberries and your cake is done, easy as pie—or should we say, "easy as cake?"—ready to slice and enjoy.

→

citrus cream cake

Serves 10   Vegetarian

For the crumb

2 cups plus
6 tablespoons/300g
all-purpose flour,
plus extra for
dusting

½ cup plus
2 tablespoons/120g
sugar

1 teaspoon baking
powder

7 tablespoons/100g
unsalted butter,
cubed, plus extra for
greasing

1 large egg, lightly
beaten

For the citrus cream

2 cups/480ml whole
milk

6 large egg yolks

¾ cup/150g sugar

¼ cup/35g all-
purpose flour

⅓ cup/35g cornstarch

3 lemons, finely
grated zest only

2 limes, finely grated
zest only

This is such a simple yet delicious recipe. A sweet, crumbly, cookie base, then a layer of zesty, citrusy cream, baked with another layer of cookie on top. The simplicity here is what makes this one of my favorites.

Start by greasing a 9-inch/23cm shallow cake pan or tart pan with a removable bottom. Once greased, lightly flour the inside of the pan.

Preheat the oven to 350°F.

To make the crumb, combine the flour, sugar, and baking powder in a large bowl. Mix till combined and then add the cubes of butter and rub them in till you no longer have large butter pieces, and your mixture looks a little like breadcrumbs. Drizzle in the beaten egg and mix it in using a rubber spatula till you have clumps of crumbs.

Spread half of the crumb mixture onto the bottom of the prepared pan till you have an even layer and press down gently. Bake for 15 minutes till the mixture is a light golden brown. Take out of the oven and let the crumb base cool completely.

Now, make the citrus cream. Pop the milk into a small pan and just gently bring to a boil. As soon as it boils, take it off the heat.

In a bowl, combine the egg yolks, sugar, flour, and cornstarch and mix till well combined. Gently drizzle in the milk in a steady flow, whisking all the time, to bring up the temperature of the eggs.

Pour the egg/milk mixture back into the pan and keep mixing on medium heat till the mixture is really thick. It may start to get thicker in clumps but keep it moving and give it a good whisk to keep it smooth. You will know it is ready when it coats the back of your spoon. Once thick, remove from the heat. Add the zest of the lemons and limes and mix well.

Spoon the mixture on top of the crumb base, leaving a ½-inch/1cm border all the way around. Level off. Take the rest of the crumb mix and add in an even layer on top and around the edge.

Pop back into the oven for 25 minutes. Once it is baked, allow to cool in the pan and then chill in the fridge for 1 hour before cutting into wedges. I love serving this with pouring cream.

marzipan plum pound

Serves 4   Vegetarian

For the cake

11¼ oz/320g store-bought pound cake

½ cup/120g unsalted butter, melted, plus extra for greasing

For the fruit

4 large plums, halved, pits can stay in

3 tablespoons sugar

1 grapefruit, finely grated zest and juice

To serve

¾ cup/250g marzipan, frozen

1 cup/100g toasted sliced almonds

Oh, my goodness, I love this recipe so much. It's the kind of thing I make when I'm chilling out on a weekend. It's simple because we're using store-bought pound cake, that I griddle, but not before it gets a good smattering of butter. It's topped off with plums, roasted in grapefruit juice and zest, and served with a grating of sweet almondy marzipan and toasted almonds.

Preheat the oven to 400°F. Lightly grease the inside of a medium roasting dish.

Put your halved plums in the dish, flat-side up, leaving the pits in. (Keeping the pits in while roasting imparts more flavor and we will get rid of them as soon as they are roasted.) Sprinkle with the sugar and add the zest and juice of the grapefruit. Bake in the oven for 20 minutes.

Now, cut the pound cake lengthwise so you have four long slices. Brush both sides with the melted butter and do this to all four.

Pop a griddle pan onto high heat and griddle the slices of cake till you have light charring on both sides. Once the plums have roasted, carefully remove their pits.

To serve, take a slice of the griddled cake, add a couple of plum halves, and drizzle with some of that grapefruit juice. Now, take your frozen marzipan and grate right on top. Sprinkle with the toasted almonds. There is no time to wait. Eat, my friends!

chapter three
RAINBOW DAYS

———

sweet potato rice paper rolls
with coconut maple dip

Serves 3–4	**Vegan/Vegetarian/Gluten-free**

For the rolls

1 lb 2 oz/500g sweet potatoes, peeled and finely grated

¼ cup/50g sugar

1 cup/100g pecans, finely chopped

¾ cup/100g raisins, finely chopped

½ teaspoon pumpkin pie spice

½ teaspoon ground cinnamon

1 orange, finely grated zest only

¼ cup/20g dried shredded coconut, toasted, plus extra for sprinkling

melted coconut oil, for greasing

12 round sheets of rice paper

For the dip

1 x 13.5-oz/400ml can of coconut cream, chilled in the fridge

¼ cup/60ml maple syrup, plus extra for drizzling

½ vanilla pod

Spring rolls are the savory fried delights that we used to get served during religious festivals. While that is all well and good, sometimes things need a little shake-up, so here I am shaking things up. These rice paper rolls are filled with a spiced sweet potato, baked, and served with a creamy coconut dip. These are *not* to be saved for special occasions, they are for whenever, wherever, every day even!

Start by making the filling. Put the grated sweet potato in a bowl. Mix in the sugar, pecans, and raisins. Now add the pumpkin pie spice, cinnamon, orange zest, and coconut and mix well. Set aside.

Lightly grease and line a baking sheet and preheat the oven to 350°F. Grab a shallow dish with sides, large enough to fit a sheet of rice paper, and fill with hot water. Also have a board ready with a clean kitchen towel placed on top to blot any excess water. Now it's time to fill and roll.

Dunk a rice paper circle into the water for 10–15 seconds, till soft. Place flat onto the board with the kitchen towel. Spoon 2 tablespoons of filling into the center, shaping into a rectangle about 3 x ¾ inch/7 x 2cm.

Fold over the bottom bit of rice paper, right over the filling. Fold over both sides and then roll till you have a neat roll. Place seam-side down onto the greased sheet and make the others. Once you have placed them all on the sheet, brush generously with the coconut oil.

Bake for 20–25 minutes, till the rolls are just crisp and the bright orange filling starts to show through. When they come out, let cool for a few minutes.

Now, it's time to make the dip. Scrape out the cold coconut cream from the can and drain off any clear liquid so you're left with just the thick cream. Put in a bowl with the maple syrup and vanilla and whisk for a few minutes, till light and fluffy. Add a few drops of warm water if it starts to split. Pop into a serving dish. If you like, drizzle with some maple syrup and sprinkle with some of that toasted coconut.

You are ready to dip and eat. Dip again and eat!

olive oil
fragrant eggs

Serves 4   Vegetarian

1 cup/240ml extra-virgin
    olive oil

1 clove of garlic, peeled
    and smashed

2 tablespoons za'atar

8 large eggs

salt

sumac, for sprinkling

4 crunchy baguettes

¾ cup/200g hummus

1 cup/20g fresh parsley

pomegranate molasses,
    for drizzling

I love cooking eggs, but as my family has grown and their appetites have grown even bigger, I can't just make a few eggs. So, this is my fast track to quick baked eggs, packed with flavor. As soon as the egg hits the oil you get beautiful frilly edges and by baking instead of frying, you get perfectly cooked whites without any slimy bits. They're flavored with za'atar, seasoned with sumac, and then finished off with a drizzle of beautifully sweet pomegranate molasses.

Start by preheating the oven to 425°F.

Pour the oil into a large roasting pan. You should have enough oil to comfortably cover the surface of the dish. To the oil add the smashed garlic, which will impart a gentle garlic flavor. Put the pan in the oven. After 6–7 minutes the oil should be smoking hot.

Sprinkle with the za'atar, which should really start sizzling. Crack in one egg at a time—they should immediately start to frill around the edges. Pop back in the oven for 3–4 minutes, until the egg whites are cooked but the centers are still runny. Take the eggs out and transfer each one gently to a plate. Sprinkle each egg with salt and a generous amount of sumac.

Split the baguettes in half lengthwise and place in the oil, flat-side down. Do this to all four and bake in the oven for a few minutes, until the oil has soaked in and the baguettes are golden brown and nicely warmed up.

Take a baguette and lather with hummus on one side. Take a quarter of the parsley (this isn't a garnish, we are using the parsley like lettuce) and pop on top of the hummus. Lay two eggs right on top and drizzle with some of the molasses. Repeat with the other baguettes. Now all that's left to do is to get your teeth around this fragrant beauty of a baguette.

crunchy okra fries

9¾ oz/280g okra	2 teaspoons salt
1¼ cups/300ml vegetable oil	1 tablespoon ground coriander
2 large egg whites	**To serve**
¾ cup/100g rice flour	any kind of mayonnaise out of a squeezy bottle
3 tablespoons curry powder	finely chopped fresh cilantro
1 tablespoon chile flakes	

Serves 4 as a snack   **Vegetarian/Gluten-free**

I love okra! Love it! It was a staple in my child-hood home, cooked simply. I like how it can be a little bit slippery but still maintain its crunch. I have been used to eating it in curry form, but oh my goodness, it is fabulous coated in crunchy spiced rice flour and baked till crisp. Everything a snack should be: flavorful, salty, and delicious. These are addictive and that's all there is to it. (You'll find photos on the next page.)

Cut the okra lengthwise down the middle, starting at the stalk end and going all the way down to the point. Take each half and slice down again—you should have four thin strips. Do this to all of them and set aside.

Preheat the oven to 425°F. Drizzle the oil on two rimmed baking sheets and put in the oven for the oil to heat up.

In a large bowl, whisk the egg whites till they are frothy. Tumble in the okra and stir until they are coated.

Now, mix the rice flour, curry powder, chile, salt, and ground coriander in a bowl. Sprinkle this dry mix all over the okra and tumble the bowl so that the okra is well coated. It might be easier to sprinkle some in and tumble, add some more, tumble, and so on, till you have no more spicy flour mix left over.

Take the sheets of hot oil out of the oven and gently add the okra in an even layer. Bake in the oven for 10 minutes. Take out, turn, and bake for 5–7 minutes, till crispy. Let cool on the sheets for a few minutes.

Transfer to a serving dish and drizzle with some mayonnaise, sprinkle some cilantro, and enjoy one of the best snacks you've ever made. There are many ways to eat okra, but this has to be my fave.   →

spinach and paneer-stuffed shells

7 oz/200g dried large pasta shells

2 tablespoons olive oil

1 tablespoon cumin seeds

2 teaspoons crushed coriander seeds

4 cloves of garlic, minced

1 onion, diced

½ teaspoon salt

2 teaspoons ground black pepper

7 oz/200g spinach, chopped

5¼ oz/150g paneer, grated

a small handful of fresh cilantro, finely chopped

3½ oz/100g cheddar cheese, grated (1 cup)

For the sauce

1⅔ cups/400g uncooked tomato purée

2 teaspoons paprika

1 lemon, finely grated zest and juice

1 teaspoon sugar

For the topping

1¾ oz/50g cheddar cheese, grated (½ cup)

3 tablespoons/20g parmesan cheese, grated

Serves 4	Vegetarian

Well, hello, let's make some room for these shells, please! A simple spicy tomato base, ginormous cooked shells, stuffed to the brim with grated paneer, spinach, and all sorts of delicious things, topped with cheese, and baked. It's like pasta shells meet lasagne and macaroni cheese. Why have one thing when you can have them all?

Start by cooking the pasta as per the instructions on the package, but cook for about 2 minutes less than the specified time, just to keep a bit of bite to the pasta. When the pasta is done, drain and run under cold water to prevent the shells from sticking.

To make the filling, add the oil to a pan and when the oil is hot, drop in the cumin and coriander seeds. As soon as they start to pop and bounce around in the pan, add the garlic and onion along with the salt and pepper. Cook for a few minutes, till the onion is just soft.

Now, throw in the spinach and cook till wilted and there is no more water in the bottom of the pan. Add that grated paneer and cook for a few minutes till it starts to get some color on it. Take off the heat, add the cilantro, and let cool for a few minutes.

Preheat the oven to 375°F.

Take a large roasting pan and pour the tomato purée into it. Add the paprika, lemon zest and juice, and sugar and give it a mix in the roasting pan.

Once the paneer mix has cooled a little, add the grated cheddar and mix well. Stuff each cooled shell with the cheese mixture and lay on top of the tomato mix.

Once you have done this to all of them, mix the cheddar and parmesan for the topping in a bowl and sprinkle right on top. Bake for 35–40 minutes, till piping hot. Remove from the oven and let cool for a few minutes before devouring. Don't judge me, but I like mine with a side of salad and all the salad cream!

seafood boil with zesty butter sauce

Serves 4   Gluten-free

For the corn and potatoes
2 whole corn on the cobs, each one cut lengthwise into 4 pieces

9 oz/250g small new potatoes, halved if large

2 lemons, halved

2 heads of garlic, halved horizontally

6 bay leaves

1 cinnamon stick

¾ cup plus 2 tablespoons /200ml olive oil

a good pinch of salt

For the seafood
1 lb 2 oz/500g fresh shrimp in shells

4 large crab claws

1 lb 2 oz/500g mussels

(or 3⅓ lb/1.5kg in total of any shellfish you like)

For the butter sauce
1 cup plus 2 tablespoons/ 250g unsalted butter

1 cup/240ml orange juice

6 cloves of garlic, minced

1 oz/30g bunch of fresh cilantro, finely chopped

2 tablespoons ground black pepper

2 tablespoons chile flakes

1 tablespoon celery salt

I had a seafood boil for the first time in Louisiana and the flavor was like nothing I had ever tasted before. It was a huge cookout for dozens of people, and quite the affair, with lots of equipment and so big it looked like it was fit for the BFG. Here I have come up with a simpler version, baked with all the deliciousness of that boil, just with less of the work. Quick-baked shellfish served with a luxurious zesty butter sauce to pour all over.

Preheat the oven to 375°F. Get two of the largest roasting pans you can find to fit in your oven.

Add the corn, potatoes, lemons, garlic, bay, and cinnamon to the pans. Drizzle with the oil. Mix well and season with the salt. Cover with foil and bake for 50 minutes.

Prepare your seafood . . .

Make the butter sauce by combining the butter, orange juice, garlic, cilantro, pepper, chile flakes, and celery salt in a pan. Mix and bring to a boil, then as soon as the butter has melted and it's just come up to a boil, lower and simmer on medium heat.

Take the pans out of the oven and add the shrimp and crab claws right on top, mixing and moving everything. Cover with foil and bake for 10 minutes. Remove from the oven, take off the foil, and drizzle with half the butter sauce. Finally, add the mussels and mix well. Leave the foil off and bake for another 10 minutes.

Take out and serve with the remaining butter sauce on the side. Get your fingers in as soon as possible and squeeze the roasted lemons of all their warm juices. Enjoy the garlic cloves that taste like garlic-flavored potatoes, the crunchy corn and soft roasted baby potatoes. Most of all, that seafood, as you patiently remove the shells that stand between you and the tender meat, covered in a buttery, citrus sauce.   →

corned beef bake

with a roasted pickle and herb oil

Serves 8–10
Gluten-free

3½ lb/1.6kg corned beef brisket, uncooked

7 tablespoons/100ml olive oil

For the roasted pickle and herb oil

1¼ cups/300ml olive oil

2 tablespoons brown mustard seeds

7 cloves of garlic, minced

2 onions, finely diced

1 green bell pepper, seeded and finely diced

12¾ oz/360g pickles, grated

2 tablespoons honey

1 lemon, juice only

2 teaspoons ground black pepper

2 tablespoons English mustard

a bunch of fresh flat-leaf parsley, finely chopped

1 cup/20g fresh cilantro, finely chopped

1¼ cups/25g fresh mint, finely chopped

To serve

broccoli

peas

green beans

I was introduced to corned beef only a few years ago. Traditionally boiled with aromatics, cooled, and sliced, it can be enjoyed in different ways. In the Irish tradition, it might be served with cabbage and potatoes, while a favorite Jewish deli–style way is to offer it stacked high on rye bread with mustard and a pickle. Both ways are delicious—and here I present it with what I view as the best of both worlds—thinly sliced and on a platter, and with mustard and pickles, which are such a perfect complement.

Take the corned beef and pat it dry of any salty moisture. You can buy good corned beef now, pre-brined for you to boil, but in this case we're baking it.

Preheat the oven to 425°F. Get a large roasting pan and pop the beef in the center. Drizzle with the oil and massage it in all over. Bake for 25 minutes.

Lower the heat to 350°F and bake for 30 minutes.

The beef should now be a gorgeous caramel color on the outside and medium-rare in the middle.

Remove the beef from the pan onto a board, cover in foil, and let rest for 30 minutes before eating and while we prepare this beautiful herby roasted oil.

Turn the oven up to 400°F. Add the oil to the roasting pan with the mustard seeds, garlic, onion, and green bell pepper. Give it all a mix and then roast for 10–12 minutes, till the onion begins to get some color on it. This should give you time to boil up your greens.

Take the roasting pan out of the oven and add the pickles, honey, lemon, pepper, and mustard and mix well. Now add all those fragrant herbs and mix well.

Lay the boiled greens on the side of a large serving dish. Slice up the beef and lay it right alongside the greens and now douse it in that herby mustard deliciousness, leaving any extra herby oil on the side if you need to go in for more.

rainbow popcorn

Serves 4–6   Vegetarian/Gluten-free

1 cup plus
    2 tablespoons/250g
    garlic butter, melted

1 tablespoon smoked
    paprika

1 teaspoon ground
    turmeric 1 tablespoon
    dried parsley, crushed
    to a powder

1 tablespoon ground
    black pepper

For the popcorn

¼ cup/50g unsalted
    butter

1½ teaspoons fine salt

⅔ cup/150g popcorn
    kernels

In recent years popcorn has become super popular as an alternative to chips. But you can enjoy what you enjoy, whether that's chips or popcorn. Some days I want chips, other days I want popcorn, and not just when I'm at the cinema. I love savory popcorn and when I can't decide on one flavor, I have all the flavors. And when I can't decide on one color, I have all the colors *and* all the flavors!

Start by melting the garlic butter until completely liquid. Divide the mixture equally among four medium bowls. To each bowl add one of the four spices/colors. Give each bowl a good mix and set the bowls aside.

Now, take a very large pot with a lid, pop on the heat, and drop in the butter and salt. As soon as the butter has melted, add the popcorn. Swirl the corn in the pan and turn up to medium to high heat.

As soon as the first kernel pops, put the lid on and let the popping commence. Every few seconds, hold the lid and swirl the whole thing on the heat, to agitate and move the corn around. The key is to listen—once the popping has totally slowed down and you can't hear any more, take it off the heat.

Take the lid off and divide the popcorn among the bowls. After each addition, mix each one well until it is covered in its tasty colors.

Have a large baking sheet at the ready and turn the oven on to 350°F.

Put the corn on the sheet one color at a time, not mixing right now but putting each batch next to each other, side by side. Pop in the oven for just 5 minutes to set the color.

Take out, mix the colors, serve up, and eat while still a little warm.

whole wheat seeded loaf
loaded with quick-fix sardines

Serves 4–6

For the loaf
3¼ cups/400g whole wheat bread flour

¾ cup/100g white bread flour

1 x ¼ oz/7g packet of fast-acting dried yeast

1 teaspoon salt

1 tablespoon molasses

1½ cups/360ml warm water

oil, for greasing

⅓ cup/50g mixed seeds

1 egg yolk

a pinch of flaky salt

For the sardines
2 large sticks of celery, finely diced

1 teaspoon salt

1 small red onion, finely diced

1 teaspoon chile flakes

a small handful of fresh cilantro

2 x 4¼ oz/120g cans of sardines in olive oil

⅓ cup/50g mixed seeds

1 lemon, for squeezing

There is nothing better than a freshly baked loaf of bread. True, I say the same about cheese, cold butter, and chips, but for now let's give fresh bread all the glory. When I make this bread, I like to serve it with my quick-fix sardines—sweet nutty bread with a spicy crunchy sardine topping.

Start by making the loaf. Combine the two flours in a large mixing bowl and mix well. Now add the yeast on one side of the bowl and the salt on the other. Give it a mix.

Add the molasses to the warm water and mix until dissolved. Make a well in the center of the dry ingredients, pour in the liquid, and mix till you can't see any more liquid.

Get your hands in and bring the dough together. If you are kneading by hand, knead for 15 minutes, till you have a dough that is smooth and elastic. If you are kneading in a stand mixer, attach the dough hook and knead for 7–8 minutes on high speed, till the dough is smooth and elastic.

Get a large bowl, lightly grease the insides, and drop the dough in there. Cover and let rise in a warm spot for about 1 hour to double in size. Lightly grease the bottom and sides of a 9 x 5-inch/900g loaf pan, at least 3 inches/7cm deep.

Once the dough has doubled in size, tip out onto a lightly floured surface and knead for a few minutes to remove any air pockets. Spread the dough flat and sprinkle all over with the mixed seeds, leaving a few teaspoons behind for the top. Push the seeds into the dough and roll the dough into a loaf shape to fit your pan.

Cover with a sheet of greased plastic wrap and let rise till doubled in size. Preheat the oven to 400°F.

Take the plastic wrap off. You will know the loaf is ready for baking if you press the dough and it springs back slowly, leaving an indent. If it doesn't leave an indent, it needs more time. Brush the top gently with the egg yolk and sprinkle with the remaining seeds and flaky salt. Bake in the oven for 40–45 minutes.

→

Once baked, let cool completely on a wire rack. Yes, it's tempting to eat it while hot and I won't stop you, but it needs that time to cool and finish cooking and to release some moisture, so I would hold off till completely cool.

Now, let's get on to making our quick-fix sardines. In a bowl, combine the celery and salt, along with the onion, chile, and cilantro. The best way to do this is to get your hands in, really squeezing the mixture. This will do two things: it will make the onion less stringent and will also soften the celery. Now, add the sardines and oil and mix everything till it's all really well combined.

To eat this, I like to take thick slices of the bread and toast it on a dry griddle to warm it up and to give it a crunch. You can also just toast it. Pile on the sardines and add a sprinkling of seeds and a little squeeze of lemon. Yum! On to the next slice now, I think . . .

chile chicken rice
with charred fava beans

2 lb 2 oz/1kg fava beans still in the pods, or frozen edamame beans, defrosted	2 tablespoons garlic paste
1 head of garlic	2 tablespoons ginger paste
3 limes, halved	2 large leeks (1 lb 9 oz/700g), thinly sliced
a pinch of salt	1 tablespoon salt
For the rice	1 lb 2 oz/500g boneless, skinless chicken thighs, thinly sliced
5–7 tablespoons/70–100g crispy chile oil	1⅓ cups/270g basmati rice
⅔ cup/100g salted peanuts	2¾ cups/650ml boiling water

Serves 6   Gluten-free

The oven does all the hard work here—no cooking rice in a pot, it's all in a roasting pan and baked. My family of rice-growing farmers may strongly disagree with this, but what is a family, really, without some tension? In our case, about how we prepare rice! This is warming with chile oil and spices, while also nutty and smoky from the charred fava beans and garlic.

Start by turning on the oven broiler to the highest possible setting.

Place the fava beans onto a baking sheet in an even layer. Break up the garlic head, remove the cloves, and scatter them right on top of the fava beans, with their skins still on. Nestle in the halved limes too.

Pop under the broiler and watch the fava beans. What you want to do is burn and char the pods. As soon as the tops of the fava beans have charred and the garlic is black (this should take 6–7 minutes), take the sheet out and use tongs to flip the fava beans so you can char the other side.

Pop back under the broiler for 5–6 minutes. Take out and, while still warm, pop everything into a zip-top food bag to sit and steam and soften. You may need two bags if you don't have one large bag.

Now, preheat the oven to 400°F and get yourself a good-sized deep roasting pan. Spoon in the crispy chile oil and add the peanuts, garlic, ginger, sliced leeks, salt, chicken, and rice and mix everything well.

Pour in the boiling water and stir everything again. Cover with foil and bake for 30 minutes.

When you have just 10 minutes left of cooking time, take the steamed garlic cloves from the bag and remove any hard pieces of garlic peel, but leave on any black charred or ashy bits. Pop all the cloves in a bowl, sprinkle with salt, and crush using the back a fork. Squeeze in the lime juice. Pod the fava beans, remove them from their skins, add to the bowl, and mix well.

Take out the chicken and rice, spoon the smoky beans and garlic into the dish, and you are ready to eat.

maple milk cake

Serves 8–10   Vegetarian

For the cake

oil, for greasing

¾ cup/100g all-purpose flour

½ teaspoon baking powder

4 large eggs

½ cup/100g sugar

For the vanilla maple milk

1 cup/240ml rice milk

3 tablespoons maple syrup

seeds scraped out from ½ vanilla pod,

For the maple cream

1½ cups/360ml good-quality maple syrup

This is like a cross between a tres leches cake and something else I concocted in my head. You know I can't leave anything alone, and this recipe is proof of that. I've taken the sweet milk-soaked sponge cake that I love from a tres leches but opted for just one type of milk instead of three and taken out the butter. It's a pillowy soft cake, which is soaked in a sweet maple and vanilla-infused rice milk, and then smothered with a thickened maple topping. What I love about this cake is that it has no butter or dairy in it, for anyone who wants a cake without these.

Start by making the cake. Preheat the oven to 375°F. Lightly grease the bottom and sides of a high 8-inch/20cm round cake pan and line the bottom with parchment paper.

Sift the flour and baking powder onto a sheet of parchment paper and set aside while you prepare the eggs and sugar.

Put the eggs and sugar into a large mixing bowl and begin whisking the mixture with electric beaters till it has tripled in volume. This can take up to 15 minutes. The mixture will become light in color and fluffy in texture. You will know the mixture is ready if you lift your whisk and it creates a trail across the mixture; the trail should be visible for 8 seconds if not longer.

Now tip the flour in, scattering it all over the surface. Using a spatula, fold the mixture gently without being too vigorous, making sure to maintain all that air and the lightness of the eggs. Keep folding gently till you have no more spots of flour.

Pour the batter into the prepared pan and put into the oven to bake on the middle shelf for 25–28 minutes.

While the cake is baking, warm the rice milk in a pan with the maple and vanilla seeds, till the maple has melted in the pan. Set aside.   →

As soon as the cake is out of the oven, drizzle with the infused milk and allow the cake to cool completely in the pan. Put it into the fridge when it is just cool.

Now, let's get on to our maple cream. I know you are going to love this recipe—I do! Pour the maple syrup into a large pot. Have a sugar thermometer ready and a bowl of ice water big enough to fit the pot of maple.

Start by boiling the maple syrup. Once it comes to a boil, cook it at a rolling boil without mixing till the temperature reaches 239°F. As soon as it does, take it off the heat and dunk the whole pan into the bowl of ice water.

Keep checking the temperature, stirring occasionally to encourage the maple syrup to cool to 212°F. As soon as the maple comes to 212°F, transfer the mixture to a bowl and whisk using electric beaters. The mixture will start to thicken and become lighter—this can take up to 20 minutes, sometimes longer. Keep at it till you have something that is thick and spreadable in consistency.

Take the cake out of the fridge and out of its pan and put straight onto a serving plate. Carefully pour or swirl the maple cream mixture right on top and you are ready to eat this beauty.

fruity baked ricotta dip

Serves 6–8   Vegetarian/Gluten-free

A good sweet dip can be considered a dessert. This one is quick and simple and uses up things you might already have at home. I love this because ricotta usually ends up in pasta or a baked cheesecake, so it's refreshing to do something a little bit different with it. Here the ricotta is mixed with zesty lemon and fragrant vanilla, with spikes of sharp passion fruit and melting chocolate. This is perfect as a simple dessert, put straight in the middle of the table with all sorts of fun things to dip. I love using chocolate-covered rice cakes, crackers, pretzels, cookies, sliced apples, and madeleines. The list could go on and on and on. (You'll find a photo on the next page.)

First, make sure you have all your bits ready that you want to serve for dipping. Chop or slice as necessary. This can be done in advance—perfect if you're having people over.

oil, for greasing

2 cups/500g ricotta

1 lemon, finely grated zest only

seeds scraped from 1 vanilla pod

2 tablespoons confectioners' sugar

3 passion fruits, halved and pulp removed

3½ oz/100g dark chocolate, chopped

½ teaspoon ground cinnamon

¼ cup/60g demerara sugar

To serve

A selection of dippers, such as chocolate-covered rice cakes, madeleines, cookies, pretzels, crackers, sliced apples, grapes, and strawberries

To make the dip, preheat the oven to 375°F. Take a shallow oven-safe pan that is about 8 inches/20cm in diameter. Grease the inside lightly.

Put the ricotta in a large bowl and give it a good mix to just help loosen it a little. Now add the lemon zest and vanilla and mix well. Add the confectioners' sugar and mix till well combined.

Add the pulp of the passion fruit and the chopped chocolate and ripple through without mixing too vigorously. Spoon the mixture into the prepared pan and smooth off the top.

Sprinkle with the cinnamon and the demerara sugar. Bake in the oven for 20 minutes, till the sugar is warm, melting, and bubbling.

Once the dip is out, give it a moment to cool, then place in the center of the table with all your edible dipping tools and devour while the dip is still warm.

→

kiwi gazpacho
with crispy coconut croissants

| Serves 4 | Vegetarian |

For the crispy coconut croissants

4 large croissants

5 tablespoons/75g coconut oil, melted

¼ cup/55g demerara sugar

1 tablespoon dried shredded coconut

For the gazpacho

8 kiwis, topped, tailed and chopped, then frozen

3 oz/80g spinach, frozen in the packaging

1¼ cups/25g fresh mint, leaves only, frozen

3 tablespoons honey, plus extra for drizzling

½ cup/50g rolled oats

1 lime, finely grated zest and juice

¾–1 cup/180–240ml apple juice

water, to thin (if needed)

1¼ cups/150g raspberries, frozen

yogurt, for drizzling

Cold soup usually isn't my jam, but a cold sweet soup most definitely is. It's a little bit like a smoothie in a bowl. This gazpacho is made from frozen kiwis and fresh mint. It's sweet, zesty, and tart and looks beautiful topped off with easy raspberry bits. Not to mention our ripped-up croissants baked in a crisp coconut sugar coating, served alongside for dipping.

What I love about this gazpacho is that you can pop all the ingredients onto a baking sheet together and freeze them overnight, ready to make this in the morning. This just means you have all the flavor of the kiwi and mint, really chilled, without adding ice that can water it down too much.

So, with everything frozen, we will begin our crispy coconut croissants.

Preheat the oven to 400°F and have a large baking sheet at the ready.

Rip the croissants into random uneven chunks and pop onto the sheet. Drizzle with the melted coconut oil and get your hands in, making sure it is all covered in the oil. This is the perfect glue to stick the sugary coconut.

In a small bowl, mix the sugar and dried coconut, then sprinkle this all over the croissants and make sure everything gets a coating. Pop in the oven and bake for 10–12 minutes, till crisp. If you like them crispier, take it further.

Now, to make our very easy gazpacho.

Put the frozen kiwi, spinach, and mint leaves into a blender with the honey, oats, lime zest, and lime juice and begin whizzing it up. Add the apple juice in a slow steady stream till you have something that resembles a thick soup/smoothie. Add a little water if you want it any thinner.

Put the frozen raspberries into a zip-top bag and crush till you have little bits. Pour your gazpacho into bowls, drizzle with some yogurt, and maybe some more honey. Sprinkle the raspberry bits.

Cold kiwi gazpacho with warm crispy coconut croissants—happy days!

coconut fish noodles

Serves 4   Gluten-free

2 tablespoons coconut oil

¼ cup/20g dried shredded coconut

2 tablespoons garlic paste

1 teaspoon ground turmeric

1 tablespoon ground black pepper

¼ cup /60ml fish sauce

1 teaspoon salt

3 lime leaves, thinly sliced

2 x 13.5-oz/400ml cans of coconut milk

8 oz/225g rice noodles

13 oz/375g cod fillets, chopped into chunks

To serve

2 large red chiles, thinly sliced

a large handful of fresh cilantro

lime wedges

This aromatic cod dish takes a few of the things I learned in Thailand and some of the influences from my own family's cooking and mixes them with one of my favorite ingredients: noodles. It's fragrant, warming, and so easy to make.

Preheat the oven to 400°F. Have a Dutch oven ready, one that has a lid.

Add the coconut oil to the Dutch oven with the dried coconut and put into the oven for the coconut to brown—this should literally only take a few minutes.

As soon as the coconut is golden, take out. Now to add the rest of your ingredients. Add the garlic, turmeric, pepper, fish sauce, salt, lime leaves, and coconut milk. Mix well.

Crush the noodles in the palm of your hand and scatter into the coconut mixture. Now add the cod chunks, put the lid on, and bake in the oven for 25 minutes, or until the noodles and fish are fully cooked through.

Give it a mix to break up the fish chunks. Spoon into bowls, scatter with some sliced red chile and cilantro, and serve with a wedge of lime.

fruit meringue pie

Serves 6–8   Vegan/Vegetarian

For the fruit

butter, for greasing

10½ oz/300g mango, diced

1 cup/200g frozen pitted cherries

⅔ cup/100g blueberries

1 tablespoon cornstarch

1¼ cups/25g fresh mint leaves

For the meringue

1 x 15-oz/425g can of chickpeas in water

1 teaspoon cream of tartar

1 cup/200g sugar

2 graham crackers

This is one of the simplest recipes, using up bits and bobs you may already have at home. Colorful fruit (I've used mango, cherries out of the freezer and blueberries, which I always have), roasted then topped off with a vegan meringue and a sprinkling of cookie crumbs, then put back in the oven to be slowly toasted. Easy-peasy!

Start by preheating the oven to 400°F.

Put the mango, cherries, and blueberries in a large, greased roasting pan and mix. Sprinkle with the cornstarch and mix well—this will soak up any juices and thicken the sauce.

Pop into the oven and bake for 25 minutes.

Meanwhile, make the meringue by straining the chickpeas and saving the water. Pop the water into a bowl with the cream of tartar and whisk with electric beaters on high for a good few minutes, until the water is white and quadrupled in size. Then start adding a small spoonful of sugar at a time, continuing to whisk and making sure to combine after each addition. Keep going till you have no more sugar left. The mixture should be smooth and glossy and should stand in stiff peaks.

Take the fruit out of the oven. Pick the mint leaves off the stalks, chop the leaves, add to the fruit, and mix well.

Lower the oven temperature to 275°F.

Dollop the meringue mixture on top, in uneven, rough peaks. Crumble the graham crackers and sprinkle all over the meringue. Bake for 1 hour 15 minutes, till the meringue is dry and crisp on the outside and chewy in the middle.

chapter four
HAPPY DAYS

Irish potato sheet pan cakes

Serves 4   Vegetarian

For the potato cakes

1 lb 2 oz/500g potatoes, peeled and diced

1⅓ cups/160g all-purpose flour, plus extra for dusting

1 teaspoon baking powder

2 teaspoons onion granules

1 teaspoon salt

For the topping

⅓ cup/90g pesto

1½ oz/40g goat cheese

3 tablespoons pine nuts

Potato cakes were one of my favorite things to buy when my kids were little. Really easy, straight out of the package, toasted and buttered, with jam some days, cheese on others, they always made for a quick and simple breakfast, lunch, dinner, or snack. As a mum of three growing kids—and as a mum who has eyes bigger than her stomach—I almost always over-cook and mashed potato is something I'm often left with. These simple beauties are a great way of using up leftover mash. They're dry-baked on a sheet pan in the oven and can be topped with all sorts of delicious goodies, like the pesto, pine nut, and goat cheese I've gone for here. Yummy!

Start by making the potato cakes. Take the peeled diced potatoes and boil till they are tender and are the perfect consistency and texture to make mash. Drain and let cool completely. Mash the potatoes and put in a large bowl.

Preheat the oven to 400°F and pop a baking sheet in the oven to warm up.

Add the flour, baking powder, onion granules, and salt to the potatoes and combine till you have a mixture that is like a dough. Don't be tempted to knead the potatoes or you'll have a potato cake that is chewy.

Dust the work surface with flour and roll out the potato dough to a 10-inch/25cm square. Cut into four equal squares and prick the potato cakes all over to prevent them from puffing up too much. Take the hot sheet out of the oven and pop the four squares straight on. You won't need oil as traditionally these are dry-fried on a flat griddle.

Bake for 15–20 minutes, till pale golden. Take out and switch the oven to broil.

While the potato cakes are still hot, spread generously with pesto, top with torn pieces of goat cheese, sprinkle with the pine nuts, and broil for a few minutes till the goat cheese is golden. Then you are ready to devour.

eggplant brioche burgers

| Serves 12 | Vegetarian |

For the brioche buns

4¾ cups/600g white bread flour

1½ teaspoons salt

1 x ¼-oz/7g fast-acting dried yeast

2 tablespoons sugar

7 tablespoons/100g unsalted butter, softened

2 large eggs, beaten

3 tablespoons tepid milk

¾ cup plus 3 tablespoons/225ml tepid water

1 egg, for glazing

2 teaspoons black sesame seeds

For the crispy eggplant

1⅔ cups/150g chickpea flour (gram flour)

1 cup plus 3 tablespoons/150g all-purpose flour

1½ teaspoons baking powder

2¼ teaspoons salt

1 teaspoon onion seeds

1 teaspoon cumin seeds

1 teaspoon coriander seeds, crushed

1 cup/240ml water

1 large egg

oil, for frying

3 eggplant, sliced into ½-inch/1cm slices

To serve

lettuce

fresh cilantro

sliced onion

mayo

mango chutney

I enjoy quite literally anything in burger form. In our house, we often eat this crispy eggplant as a snack but it is even nicer sandwiched in a soft buttery brioche bun—the superior bun where burgers are concerned. The buns are simple to bake and worth it to make the best burgers. If you don't want all 12 straight away they can be frozen.

Start by making the brioche dough. Put the flour and salt in a large bowl with the yeast and sugar and mix well.

Add the butter, then get your hands in and rub in the butter till you have a mixture that looks like breadcrumbs. Make a well in the center, add the eggs and milk, and mix well. Gently pour in the water and mix with your hands till you have a dough.

Now, tip the dough out and knead till it is smooth, elastic, and very stretchy. Pop into a bowl, cover, and let rise for 3 hours in the fridge.

Take the dough out and knead again for a few minutes. Divide the mixture into 12 equal dough balls. Have two baking sheets ready, both lightly greased and lined with parchment paper. Place 6 dough balls on each sheet, leaving some room for the dough balls to grow. Cover with greased plastic wrap and let rise till doubled in size.

Preheat the oven to 400°F. Uncover the dough balls, brush the tops with egg, and sprinkle with the black sesame seeds. Bake for 20–25 minutes. →

While the brioche buns bake, make the crispy eggplant. Combine the flours, baking powder, salt, onion seeds, cumin, and coriander seeds in a bowl and mix well. Pour in the water and egg and whisk till you have a smooth batter.

Add oil to a shallow frying pan, dip the eggplant slices into the batter, and gently fry for 6 minutes on each side. Drain on paper towels.

As soon as the buns have come out of the oven, let cool for 10 minutes, then cut in half. To build your burgers, add lettuce, cilantro, sliced onion, mayo, and eggplant, topped with mango chutney, into the buns, and there you have it—a deliciously crisp eggplant burger in a sweet brioche bun.

thai red mussel omelet with oven-baked fries

Serves 4–6

For the fries

1 lb 10 oz/750g russet potatoes, peeled and sliced into fry batons

2 tablespoons salt

½ cup/120ml vegetable oil

1 tablespoon all-purpose flour

1 teaspoon cornstarch½ teaspoon baking powder

For the omelet

2 x 4.2 oz/120g cans of mussels

1 red onion, thinly sliced

3 tablespoons Thai red curry paste

6 large eggs, lightly beaten

a pinch of salt

fresh cilantro

While I like anything fried, especially fries, I always get asked if I can do a recipe for oven fries, so here it is. While I admit it's not quite as easy as emptying a bag from the freezer onto a sheet and whacking it in the oven, this recipe is far tastier. One of the things I love to eat with fries is an omelet and this Thai red mussel omelet is a particular favorite of mine.

Start by soaking your prepped potato batons in water for at least 1 hour.

Once soaked, pop them into a large pot with fresh water, add the salt, and mix. Bring to a boil and then boil for 2–3 minutes, till just tender. Drain and allow to dry off a little on a few sheets of paper towel.

Preheat the oven to 400°F. Pour the vegetable oil into a rimmed baking sheet and pop into the oven for the oil to get hot.

Meanwhile, mix together the flour, cornstarch, and baking powder. Toss the par-cooked batons in the dry mixture till they are entirely coated. Take the sheet with the hot oil out of the oven and carefully pop in the fries in an even layer. Use tongs to coat each side of the fries in the hot oil and then bake in the oven for 50–60 minutes. Be sure to turn the fries halfway through cooking. Ten minutes before the end of the fry cooking time, start on that omelet.

Take some of the oil from the canned mussels and pop into a large frying pan on the stove. As soon as the oil is hot, add the onion and cook for about 5 minutes, till the onion is just soft.

Stir in the paste and warm through. Add the mussels, eggs, and a pinch of salt and mix till the egg just starts to set. As soon as the top sets, flip it over.

The fries should be ready at the same time as the omelet. Be sure to season the fries well, sprinkle with cilantro, and enjoy your oven-baked fries and omelet.

breakfast yorkie

2 large eggs, fridge-cold

½ cup plus
1 tablespoon/70g
white bread flour

7 tablespoons/100ml
whole milk, fridge-cold

3 tablespoons clarified
butter (ghee)

⅓ cup/40g granola,
without fruit, plus a
little extra to sprinkle

For the topping

2 large oranges,
segmented

1 tablespoon
marmalade

1 tablespoon
confectioners' sugar

This is inspired by the German pancakes I had when I was out in Berlin. Texture-wise they were very much like a Yorkshire pudding, but sweet and served with confectioners' sugar and syrup. So, I have re-created my version of exactly what I loved about that breakfast: Yorkshire pudding batter, crisp in places, soft in others, crunchy with granola and zesty with marmalade and oranges.

Start by making the batter. Combine the eggs, flour, and milk in a bowl and, using an immersion blender, whiz the mixture till it is thick, even, and lump-free. Give the bowl a good few bangs on the worktop to get rid of any air bubbles. Pop the mixture into the fridge for at least 10 minutes, to rest.

Meanwhile, preheat the oven to 450°F and pop in an 8-inch/20cm cast-iron pan or cake pan to heat up with the clarified butter. The pan should be hot and the butter should be really very hot before pouring the batter in.

Have the batter and your granola ready. Take the very hot pan out of the oven and leave the oven door open. Pour the batter in, sprinkle with the granola and bake for 12–18 minutes, till the batter has risen and is crisp and brown around the edges and softer in the center.

While it's baking, put the orange segments in a small pan, squeezing out any remaining juice. Add the marmalade and gently warm through.

As soon as the large yorkie is out, spread the warm orange marmalade and segments over the top, sprinkle with extra granola, dust with confectioners' sugar, and it is ready to eat.

cheese beignets

Makes 24   Vegetarian

For the puffs

7 tablespoons/100g unsalted butter, plus extra for greasing

1¼ cups/300ml water

2 teaspoons sugar

1 cup plus 3 tablespoons/150g all-purpose flour

2 teaspoons mixed dried herbs

4 large eggs, lightly beaten

2¼ oz/60g cheddar cheese, finely grated (½ cup)

1½ oz/40g parmesan cheese, finely grated (⅓ cup)

⅔ cup/70g mixed grated cheese, for rolling

For the balsamic bean dip

1 x 15-oz/425g can of baked beans, drained

1 tablespoon olive oil

2 tablespoons balsamic vinegar

a pinch of salt

1 teaspoon ground black pepper

1 teaspoon paprika

These are my absolute favorite. Made with a cheesy dough that then gets rolled in even more cheese, they are light, irresistible, and baked to perfection. I love them served with this simple balsamic bean dip.

Start by making the cheese puffs. Combine the butter and water in a medium pot along with the sugar. Pop onto medium heat and bring to a boil. Meanwhile, mix the flour and mixed herbs together.

As soon as the water comes to a boil and the butter has melted, quickly pour the herby flour into the butter mixture and stir over low heat till you have no patches of flour left. Continue to mix for at least 5 minutes to really cook the flour.

Transfer the dough to a stand mixer bowl and let cool for 5 minutes. With the mixer on low speed, add the egg a little at a time. Continue to mix on low. It will look like it's not coming together, but it will, just keep mixing. Do this till you have a smooth, soft dough with a similar consistency to room-temperature butter. You may not need all the egg. (If you don't have a stand mixer, you can mix by hand, but make sure the dough is taken off the heat, transferred out of the hot pot, and allowed to cool a little before starting to add the egg.)

Now, let cool completely in the bowl. As soon as it has completely cooled, add the cheddar and parmesan and mix till they are all evenly dispersed.

Preheat the oven to 425°F and have a baking sheet lightly greased and lined with parchment paper.

Form the dough into balls, each about 2 teaspoons' worth, and roll in the mixed grated cheese until entirely covered. Pop onto the sheet.

Once you have rolled them all, bake in the oven for 23–25 minutes, till crisp and golden on the outside.

While they bake, make the easy balsamic bean dip. In a food processor, blend the beans, oil, balsamic, salt, pepper, and paprika till you have a smooth dip. Add a splash of water to make it more of the consistency of a dip.

Serve the beignets with the dip alongside.

cornbread dog

Serves 6

oil, for greasing

12 oz/340g small cocktail sausages

3 cups/375g all-purpose flour

1⅓ cups/225g polenta or coarsely ground cornmeal

1 teaspoon salt2 teaspoons garlic granules

4 teaspoons baking powder

¼ cup/50g sugar

2 cups/480ml whole milk

2 large eggs

½ cup/110g unsalted butter, melted

squeezy ketchup

squeezy mustard

I have to admit that I've never eaten an authentic corn dog. I've seen them in movies, cartoons, and extreme food shows, but I am yet to get my hands on one. So, I decided it was time to make my own family-friendly version, creating as little washing-up as possible, but still with all the elements of a corn dog: delicious soft cornbread, a layer of sausages in the center, and topped off with mustard and ketchup.

Preheat the oven to 400°F and drizzle oil into a 9-inch/23cm square cake pan. Add the Vienna sausages and bake till golden brown. Take out and transfer to a plate. Add a little extra oil, brush all over the bottom and sides of the pan and set aside.

Make the corn dog batter by combining the flour, polenta, salt, garlic, baking powder, and sugar in a large bowl and stirring till well combined.

Make a well in the center and add the liquid ingredients: the milk, eggs, and melted butter go straight in. Whisk until you have a well-combined, thick mixture.

Pour half the mixture into the prepared pan and level off the surface. Layer in the sausages, then pour in the rest of the batter and level off. Drizzle with ketchup and mustard and bake for 40–45 minutes.

Let cool in the pan for 10 minutes. Cut into squares and you should have a yummy layer of sausage surrounded by a delicious corny batter. Serve with ketchup and mustard.

paprika egg filo bake

Serves 4	**Vegetarian**

9½ oz/270g filo pastry (7 sheets)

½ cup/125g unsalted butter, melted

4 large eggs

2 green onions, thinly sliced

a small handful of fresh cilantro, thinly sliced

2 teaspoons smoked paprika

1 teaspoon salt

sriracha

This is so simple and easy to make, but it looks glorious, with its swirls of buttered filo, baked till crisp, and a set eggy filling flavored with smoked paprika and a hit of sriracha to finish it off. It's like having a slice of a savory tart, but more beautiful and a lot less work.

Preheat the oven to 425°F and take an 8-inch/20cm round roasting pan.

Brush a filo sheet generously all over with butter and roll up lengthwise. Curl this up loosely like a snail's shell, swirling it all the way around, and pop into the center of the pan.

Do the same to another sheet, brushing, rolling, and loosely swirling it around the swirl of filo already in the pan. Keep doing this with each sheet, wrapping as you go till you have used up all the pastry. The swirl of rolled-up filo sheets should fill the pan to the edges.

Bake in the oven for 10 minutes, until crisp and golden.

Meanwhile, make the filling by combining the eggs in a bowl with the green onion, cilantro, paprika, and salt and mixing well.

Pour the mixture all over the baked filo. Drizzle with the sriracha and bake for 13–15 minutes. Take out and let cool for 15 minutes before slicing and eating.

dump-it-all-in Mexican dinner

Serves 6

4 large tortillas, sliced into strips

¼ cup/60ml oil

2 lb 2 oz/1kg ground lamb

¼ cup/55g garlic paste

2 onions, finely diced

2 teaspoons salt

2 tablespoons ground cumin

1 tablespoon ground coriander

1 tablespoon chile flakes

2 tablespoons tomato paste

1 x 14-oz/400g can of diced tomatoes

3 tablespoons Worcestershire sauce

To serve

7 oz/200g cheddar cheese, grated (1¾ cups)

1 x 15-oz/425g can of sliced jalapeños, drained

sour cream

guacamole

thinly sliced fresh cilantro

lime wedges

This is the kind of meal that saves my rear end when I am in a rush or just need a quick dinner. The clue is in the name. It's a dump-it-all-in-style dish of simply spiced cooked meat, mixed with crisp tortilla strips, baked with cheese and jalapeño. Easy, simple, and delicious.

Preheat the oven to 400°F.

Place the tortilla strips on a baking sheet. Drizzle with the oil and bake in the oven for 15 minutes, till the strips are golden. Keep the oven on.

Take the strips out and set aside. Start browning the ground lamb on the stove in a large Dutch oven. Once browned, remove with a slotted spoon onto a plate and set aside.

Pour a little more oil into the pan. As soon as the oil is hot, add the garlic and cook for just long enough to brown it slightly. Add the onion and salt and cook till the onion is soft and golden.

Now for the spices. Add the cumin, coriander, and chile flakes and cook for 1 minute before adding the tomato paste, tomatoes, and Worcestershire sauce. Cook for 10 minutes. Add the meat and cook with the lid off till the meat is cooked and the sauce has thickened.

Now, add the toasted tortilla chips and mix well, leaving a few of those crispy bits to poke out.

Sprinkle with cheese and jalapeños and bake in the oven for 20 minutes, till the cheese is oozy. Take out, dollop sour cream and guacamole on top, sprinkle with cilantro, squeeze in some lime juice, and add the wedges and you are ready to eat your dump-it-all-in-the-pan Mexican dinner!

southern "fried" chicken livers

¾ cup/100g all-purpose flour

2 teaspoons garlic powder

2 teaspoons paprika

2 teaspoons dried thyme

1½ teaspoons salt

2 teaspoons ground black pepper

2 large egg whites

1¾ lb/800g chicken livers

¾ cup plus 2 tablespoons/200ml oil

To serve

pan-fried greens

mashed potatoes

Scotch bonnet pepper sauce

Serves 4

I grew up eating offal, so meals like this are on my table at home every few days, and I sometimes find myself craving chicken livers like I do chocolate! There is something nourishing about their rich iron taste and creamy texture. These are my crispy southern-fried-style livers, baked in the oven for ease. Move over, fried chicken!

Start by mixing up the coating. Put the flour in a bowl with the garlic powder, paprika, thyme, and 1 teaspoon each of the salt and black pepper. Mix well, spread onto a wide plate, and set aside.

Now, take the egg whites and whisk them till they are just frothy. Add the remaining salt and pepper and give it another quick whisk.

Use a piece of paper towel to pat the chicken livers dry. Drop the chicken livers into the frothy egg whites and mix well till evenly coated.

Preheat the oven to 400°F. Pour the oil on a rimmed baking sheet and put the sheet into the oven to allow the oil to get really hot.

Take each piece of liver coated in the seasoned egg white and pat into the dry seasoning mix. Do this to each piece individually till you have coated every single one. If you have any seasoning left, coat each one again till you have used it all.

Carefully take the sheet out of the oven and put the livers on one by one. Turn them so they are fully coated in the hot oil, then bake in the oven for 12–15 minutes. Make sure to turn them halfway through the cooking time.

When they come out, they should be crisp and well-seasoned on the outside and creamy on the inside. Serve with quick pan-fried greens, mash, and tons of Scotch bonnet sauce.

mushroom carnitas

Serves 3–4	**Vegetarian**

This vegetarian take on Mexican carnitas is made with portobello mushrooms cooked with garlic and thyme and baked till crisp. Served in a toasted pita (instead of the traditional tortilla) and topped with a pickled beet mayo, these are so simple and need very little else.

Preheat the oven to 400°F and add the oil to a rimmed baking sheet or large baking pan.

Add the minced garlic and mushrooms. Stir so that all the mushrooms are coated. Bake in the oven for 40 minutes, being sure to take out and mix at regular intervals so everything crisps up evenly. About 15 minutes before the mushrooms are finished, add the sprig of thyme.

7 tablespoons/100ml oil

3 cloves of garlic, minced

1 lb 2 oz/500g portobello mushrooms, thinly sliced into baton strips

a large sprig of fresh lemon thyme

3–4 pita breads

For the mayo

1 cup/220g shredded pickled beet, drained and excess vinegar removed

1 cup/240g full-fat mayo

a large handful of thinly sliced fresh chives

Meanwhile, make the beet mayo by combining the beet in a bowl with the mayo and sliced chives and mixing well.

Just before the mushrooms are finished, pop the pitas right on top till they are toasted and puffed up. As soon as they are, take the sheet out and remove the pitas from the top.

Take out the thyme stalk, remove any leaves, and mix them into the mushrooms. Cut open the pitas. Fill and top with the mushrooms and mayo and you are so ready to take a bite!

rhubarb, rose, and strawberry bake with a scone top

For the base

1 vanilla pod

9 oz/250g fresh or frozen rhubarb, chopped if fresh

14 oz/400g strawberries, halved

1 teaspoon rose water

2 tablespoons water

3 organic roses, petals only, plus extra for decoration

For the scones

1¾ cups plus 1 tablespoon/225g all-purpose flour, sifted

2½ teaspoons baking powder

½ teaspoon salt

4 cardamom pods, black seeds crushed to a powder

¼ cup/55g unsalted butter, cubed, plus extra for greasing

2 tablespoons granulated sugar

½ cup/120ml whole milk

1 egg, beaten, for glazing

demerara sugar, for sprinkling

To serve

chopped pistachios

rose petals

clotted cream or crème fraîche

Serves 4–6   Vegetarian

This is one of the coolest and easiest recipes ever, bringing lots of things I love together in one place: tart rhubarb, scented rose, and sweet strawberries, all topped with scones. Like an afternoon tea but in dessert form, which frankly is all the motivation I ever need to make this recipe!

Preheat the oven to 375°F. Lightly grease a round roasting pan, approx. 10 inches/25cm in diameter.

Split the vanilla pod and scrape out the seeds into the pan. Add the rhubarb, strawberries, rose water, and water and mix well. Pop into the oven and bake for 20 minutes. Once removed from the oven, add the rose petals and mix them into the hot fruit. Keep the oven turned on and increase the heat to 400°F.

Meanwhile, make the scone mix. Put the flour in a bowl with the baking powder, salt, cardamom pods, butter, and sugar and use your fingers to rub the butter into the flour mix. Make a well in the center and add the milk. Using your hands, bring the dough together, but do this without kneading or you will get a tough, chewy dough.

On a well-floured surface, roll out the dough to a circle of 10 inches/25cm and cut into six equal triangles. Place on top of the rhubarb mixture. Brush the top of each scone triangle with beaten egg and sprinkle generously with the crunchy demerara.

Put back into the oven for 20–25 minutes. Take out and let cool for 10 minutes then sprinkle with the chopped pistachios and rose petals and serve with clotted cream. →

ultimate nut butter-stuffed cookies

Makes 15   Vegetarian

cooking spray

15 heaped teaspoons almond butter

½ cup/115g unsalted butter, softened

packed ¾ cup plus 1 tablespoon/175g brown sugar

1 large egg

1 teaspoon almond extract

2¼ cups/275g all-purpose flour

½ teaspoon baking soda

½ teaspoon salt

1 tablespoon cornstarch

¾ cup/100g roasted finely chopped almonds

These are my husband's absolute favorite; he loves nuts in any form. The cookies are soft, with nuts in the dough, and best of all they have a melt-in-the-mouth center of oozy nut butter.

Take an ice-cube tray and grease the inside with some cooking spray. Fill 15 wells with 1 heaped teaspoon each of the nut butter and freeze for at least 1 hour. Take them out of the tray and roll into balls, then pop onto a plate and back into the freezer.

Make the dough by combining the butter and sugar in a bowl and mixing till light and fluffy. Add the egg and almond extract and mix well.

Now add the dry ingredients—the flour, baking soda, salt, cornstarch, and almonds—and mix till you have a dough mixture. Divide into 15 equal balls.

Take the frozen almond butter out of the freezer. Take each dough ball, flatten, add a frozen ball of nut butter into the center, and wrap the dough around the butter, making sure there are no holes. Pop onto a plate and into the freezer for 30 minutes.

Preheat the oven to 400°F and lightly grease and line three baking sheets.

Place five dough balls onto each sheet, leaving space for them to spread as they bake. Bake in the oven for 12–14 minutes.

Take out and let cool completely on the sheets and then they are ready to eat. Make a cup of tea and break a cookie in half to reveal that nutty center.

crunchy nut corn flake tart

Serves 6   Vegetarian

For the pastry

½ cup plus 2 tablespoons/150g unsalted butter, cubed

2 cups plus 6 tablespoons/300g all-purpose flour

½ vanilla pod, seeds scraped out

a pinch of salt

water, as needed

For the filling

6 tablespoons/125g raspberry jam

¼ cup/60g unsalted butter

7 tablespoons/100ml golden syrup or light corn syrup

2 tablespoons brown sugar

3⅔ cups/150g honey nut corn flakes

3 tablespoons salted peanuts, roughly chopped

hot custard, to serve

This old-school classic was on the menu every day when I used to line up for school dinners. I fondly remember its crisp—or sometimes soggy!—pastry, raspberry jam, and a syrupy-sweet corn flake filling. All served with hot custard on top. Here I have re-created the same recipe but of course with a few tweaks of my own!

Start by making the pastry. Put the butter in a bowl with the flour, vanilla seeds, and salt. Rub the butter into the flour till there are no more clumps of butter left. Add a few tablespoons of water to the dough, as needed, and gently bring the dough together into a ball. Wrap in plastic wrap, flatten, and chill in the fridge for 30 minutes.

Preheat the oven to 400°F and have a 9-inch/23cm fluted tart pan with a removable bottom at the ready.

Take the pastry out and, on a lightly floured surface, roll out large enough for the pastry to cover the bottom and sides of the tart pan, with a little bit of an overhang.

Prick the bottom of the tart with a fork. Line the inside with some parchment paper. Fill with baking beads or dried lentils/rice and blind bake for 15 minutes. Remove the tart from the oven. Take out the paper and beads/lentils/rice and bake for 10 minutes.

As soon as the tart shell is out, spread a generous amount of the jam all across the bottom. Now, melt the butter, syrup, and sugar in a large pot. As soon as the butter has melted, add the cereal. Mix till everything is coated and glossy.

Tip right onto the jam in an even layer. Sprinkle with the peanuts and pop back into the oven for 5 minutes.

Take out and now trim off the excess pastry while it is still warm, then let cool completely in the pan as this will help to really set the cereal. Cut into wedges when cold and serve with hot custard. School desserts all over again, but a little bit better and we can even go back for seconds!

chocolate cookie pie

Serves 12–16
Vegetarian

For the cookie dough

¾ cup plus 2 tablespoons/200g unsalted butter, softened, plus extra for greasing

packed 1½ cups/325g brown sugar

2 large eggs, plus 1 large egg yolk

1 teaspoon vanilla extract

1 teaspoon almond extract

3⅓ cups/425g all-purpose flour, sifted

1½ teaspoons baking soda

½ teaspoon salt

2¼ cups/400g dark chocolate chips

For the filling

2½ cups/750g chocolate hazelnut spread

1⅓ cups/200g roasted chopped hazelnuts

7 oz/200g chocolate-covered wafer cookies, chopped into cubes

This cookie pie is exactly what it says in the name: a deep-filled pie made with cookie dough "pastry," filled with chocolate wafer bars, hazelnuts, and chocolate spread. It's indulgent, decadent, fun, and all-around delicious. Come on, let's stop talking and make this thing already.

Start by making the dough. Put the butter in a large bowl with the sugar and beat till the mixture is light and creamy. Add the egg, egg yolk, vanilla, and almond and incorporate well.

Now add the dry ingredients—the flour, baking soda, and salt—and mix till you have a stiff cookie dough. Add the chocolate chips and make sure they are evenly dispersed into the dough.

Divide the mixture into two-thirds for the bottom and sides and a third for the top. Lightly grease and line the bottom of a 9-inch/23cm springform pan. Take the large ball of dough and gently roll out on a lightly floured surface so it is large enough to fit the bottom and sides of the cake pan, with a tiny bit of overhang to connect the top of the pie. Press it into the pan.

Take the chocolate hazelnut spread and mix with the roasted hazelnuts. Add half the mixture to the lined cookie dough pan. Top with the chopped chocolate-covered wafer cookies, then top with the rest of the chocolate spread mix and level off.

Take the small bit of cookie dough that is left over and roll out to the size of the top. With a little water on your finger, just dampen the top of the cookie dough around the top edge. Pop the top of the pie on and pinch the edges to seal. Cut off any excess. Now chill the whole thing in the freezer for 1 hour.

Preheat the oven to 375°F.

Bake the pie in the oven for 25–30 minutes, till the dough is golden. Take out of the oven and let cool completely in the pan. I hate to say this to you, but you still can't eat this. We must wait for it to chill in the fridge completely overnight. I promise it's worth the wait. Loosen the pie from the pan by releasing the sides before chilling or it becomes very difficult to remove.

Take out of the pan after your long wait, cut into wedges, and enjoy with a cup of tea. Or even better yet, enjoy on a picnic!

→

happy days

chapter five
BAKING DAYS

coffee cake
with dalgona coffee cream

Serves 6–8   Vegetarian

For the cake

¾ cup/175g unsalted butter, softened, plus extra for greasing

packed ¾ cup plus 1 tablespoon/175g brown sugar

3 large eggs

1⅓ cups plus 1 tablespoon/175g all-purpose flour

1 tablespoon baking powder

¼ teaspoon salt

2 teaspoons freeze-dried instant coffee

1 tablespoon hot water

For the dalgona coffee cream

2 tablespoons instant coffee

5 tablespoons/65g granulated sugar

5 tablespoons/75ml boiling water

cocoa powder, for sprinkling

If anyone says you can't have cake for breakfast, you can tell them I sent you! My kids will back me up: anyone can have cake for breakfast, especially if it's coffee cake! This is a sweet and intense cake and there is no hiding from the coffee flavor. It's topped with a dalgona cream—yes, you guessed right—more coffee!

This is a very simple cake. It should be almost as quick as making a pot of coffee, with just a tiny bit of extra work.

Start by preheating the oven to 350°F. Grease and line the bottom and sides of an 8-inch/20cm round cake pan with a removable bottom.

Put the butter and sugar in a bowl with the eggs, flour, baking powder, and salt. Combine the coffee and hot water and mix well. Add to the cake mixture.

Now, beat everything till you have a smooth, shiny cake batter. This should take 2–3 minutes. Pour the mixture into the pan and level off the top.

Bake for 35–40 minutes, till a skewer inserted comes out clean. Take out and let cool in the pan for 10 minutes. Remove from the pan and completely cool on a cooling rack.

Make the dalgona cream by combining the instant coffee, sugar, and boiling water and whisking with electric beaters for a few minutes, till light and fluffy. Pour or swirl on top of the cooled cake. Sprinkle with a little cocoa and you are ready for your morning brew, in cake form!

eat-later honey cake

Serves 9   Vegetarian

½ cup plus 2 tablespoons/150ml hot water

3 Earl Grey tea bags

7 tablespoons/100ml vegetable oil

2 large eggs

packed ¼ cup/50g brown sugar

½ cup/120ml golden syrup or light corn syrup

2 tablespoons molasses

1¾ cups plus 1 tablespoon/225g all-purpose flour, sifted

1 teaspoon baking powder

1 teaspoon ground cinnamon

1 teaspoon ground ginger

1 teaspoon pumpkin pie spice

1½ cups/200g pine nuts

Honey cake is one of my all-time favorites to make and eat. One of the reasons why I like it so much is that it gets tastier the longer it rests. The funniest thing is that there is, in fact, no honey in the cake, despite the name. My nan used to think the honey in the UK was tastier than anything she had tried in her life; turns out she was eating golden syrup the whole time! To make this cake even more delicious, I let it rest wrapped in paper and foil for up to 1 week for out-of-this-world gooeyness. While I usually have very little patience, where this cake is involved, I somehow manage to find plenty.

Start by preheating the oven to 350°F. Grease and line a 9-inch/23cm square cake pan.

Pour the hot water into a liquid measuring cup and add the tea bags. Mix till you have a dark liquid, then remove the tea bags. Be sure not to squeeze the tea bags or the mixture will become bitter. If you don't have ½ cup plus 2 tablespoons/150ml of tea, just top up with hot water till you do. Pour the oil into the measuring cup and set aside.

Put the eggs, sugar, golden syrup, and molasses into a mixing bowl and whisk till you have a mixture that is light and fluffy. Pour in the oil and tea mixture.

Put the flour, baking powder, cinnamon, ginger, and pumpkin pie spice in another bowl and mix together. Pour the wet ingredients into the dry ingredients and stir till you have a thick cake batter.

Sprinkle half the pine nuts into the bottom of the cake pan. Pour in the cake batter, making sure the top is level. Sprinkle with the rest of the pine nuts and bake for 40 minutes.

Take the cake out and allow to cool in the pan completely.

Cut the cake into squares, then lift it out of the pan, still in the paper, and straight onto a piece of foil. Cover the top with another layer of foil and paper. Wrap tightly and let rest at room temperature for ideally at least 1 week before eating (or 4 days will suffice if you're short on patience). When you unwrap, you should have a rich, gooey cake, sweet and deep in flavor, which sticks to the roof of your mouth!

no-knead bread

Makes 1 loaf   Vegan/Vegetarian

4 cups/500g white bread flour, plus extra for dusting

1 x ¼-oz/7g packet of fast-acting dried yeast

1 teaspoon salt

1 teaspoon sugar

1½ cups/360ml warm water

oil, for greasing

We all *need* a recipe for a no-*knead* dough! See what I did there? Never mind! I have days when I bake almost non-stop and this is a go-to recipe for me as it's super easy, with absolutely no kneading. The method is the kind that involves a bit of stop and start, but as the dough rises gently, the flavor develops, making for an incredibly delicious loaf.

Find a large container that's small enough to fit in your fridge. Put the flour in the container, along with the yeast, salt, and sugar, and mix really well. Pour in the water and mix until you have no floury bits.

Cover with plastic wrap, leaving a small gap for the gases to escape, and put in a warm place for as long as it takes for the dough to double in size. As soon as it has, pop into the fridge overnight.

Have a baking sheet ready, lightly greased and lined with some parchment paper. This is the sheet on which we will bake our free-form bread dough. Take the dough out of the fridge and lightly flour the work surface. Tip the dough out onto it.

Knock the air out and flatten the dough. Tuck in the ends, into the center, turn the dough around, seam-side down, and pop onto the sheet. Cover with plastic wrap and let rise till an indent made in the dough stays there and only comes back up slowly.

Preheat the oven to 425°F. Pop a roasting pan in the bottom of the oven and fill with hot water. This is to create steam, which will give the loaf a chewy crust.

Uncover the dough, slash the top in three places, and bake for 25–30 minutes. You will know the bread is baked if, when tapped underneath, the loaf sounds hollow. Let cool completely on a cooling rack. Slice and enjoy with good cold butter and pinches of flaky salt.

peppery black olive palmiers

Makes about 35

The sweet versions of these palmiers (or "elephants' ears," as we like to call them) are my mum's favorite, but you can make them any which way you want. Once you have mastered a simple rough puff pastry, what you put into them is up to you. Here I'm going savory and filling them with salty black olive tapenade, lots of pepper, and some cheese. Simple and delicious.

Start by making the rough puff pastry. Put the flour in a bowl with the chives and salt. Mix well. Add the cubed butter and get your hands in, rubbing the butter into the flour in chunks. We are not looking to get rid of the butter completely in the flour, we want chunks of butter still remaining so that when the butter melts, we get an uneven layering of pastry.

As soon as you have roughly rubbed the butter into the flour, make a well in the center. Pour in the water and bring the dough together. Shape into a flat rectangle, wrap in plastic wrap, and chill for 30 minutes in the fridge.

For the rough puff

2 cups/250g white bread flour, plus extra for dusting

3 tablespoons chopped fresh chives

1 teaspoon salt

1 cup plus 2 tablespoons/250g unsalted butter, just soft, cubed, plus extra for greasing

7 tablespoons/100ml cold water

1 egg, lightly beaten

For the filling

3 tablespoons black olive tapenade

1 tablespoon ground black pepper

1¾ oz/50g parmesan cheese, finely grated (6 tablespoons)

Flour the surface and roll the pastry out to an 8 x 16-inch/20 x 40cm rectangle. With the long end closest to you, fold the leftmost third of the pastry onto the center third and then fold the rightmost third over the top. You should now have three layers of pastry.

Roll out to 8 x 12 inches/20 x 30cm, with the longest side closest to you, then fold in thirds again. Roll out again to 8 x 12 inches/20 x 30cm and repeat the folding one more time. Wrap and pop into the fridge for 30 minutes.

Have two baking sheets ready, lightly greased and lined. Mix the filling by combining the tapenade, pepper, and parmesan and mixing well. Take the pastry out and, on a lightly floured surface, roll a rectangle of 16 x 12 inches/40 x 30cm.

Spread the top with the filling mixture. Orient the longest side closest to you. Roll this side inward away from you, rolling tightly till you get to the center. Now do the same for the other long edge till it meets in the center.

Where they meet in the middle and connect, brush lightly with some beaten egg and gently push the two sides together to seal. Pop into the freezer for 30 minutes.

Preheat the oven to 400°F. Take the roll out of the freezer and cut into roughly ½-inch/1cm slices, trimming off any ragged or uneven bits from the two ends of the roll. Place the slices on their sides on the prepared sheets. Brush with beaten egg and bake for 20–25 minutes, till crisp and golden.

Take the palmiers out and allow to cool completely on the sheets before enjoying with a cold drink.

baked feta
with chile, honey, and thyme

Serves 6   Vegetarian

14 ox/400g feta cheese

¼ cup/60ml olive oil, plus extra for greasing

a large sprig of fresh lemon thyme, stemmed

1 teaspoon dried oregano

1 teaspoon chile flakes

7 oz/200g salted crisp crackers

honey, for drizzling

slices of crusty bread, to serve

Except for me, not one soul in my house likes feta, so I make this recipe all for myself and my sisters. Baked with herbs and chile, and served with a drizzle of honey, this feta is salty, sweet, spicy, and herby, making for the most delicious warm dip that really does everything.

Preheat the oven to 400°F. Lightly grease a small roasting pan.

Put the feta cheese right into the pan and drizzle generously with the oil. Sprinkle with the thyme, oregano, and chile. Cover with foil and bake for 25 minutes. For the last 5 minutes of baking, put the crackers on a baking sheet in the oven and warm through.

Take the foil off the feta and drizzle with honey. Get your warm crackers out and spread with the warm, salty, sweet, herby feta. Mop up that oil with warm crusty bread.

crunch wrap

Serves 6

chile oil, for greasing

8 large flour tortillas

⅔ cup/300g mango chutney

1¾ cups/200g shredded mozzarella

1 lb/450g ground lamb

6 tablespoons/100g plain yogurt

2 tablespoons curry powder

2 red onions, thinly sliced

8 oz/225g paneer, grated

1 teaspoon garlic powder

1 teaspoon chile powder

8 poppadoms

a large handful of fresh cilantro

This is such a simple and easy bake, made with ingredients I usually have knocking about the house. Baking doesn't have to be laborious or time-consuming and this is the kind of thing you can just put together: tortilla wraps filled with all sorts of goodies—chutney, ground meat, onions, paneer, and poppadoms for crunch—and baked to simple perfection.

Start by generously greasing a 9 x 13-inch/23 x 33cm baking pan. Preheat the oven to 375°F.

Grease seven large tortillas with the chile oil. Start lining the pan with the tortillas, greased-side down. Place a tortilla on each of the shorter ends of the pan, leaving some of the tortilla hanging over the edge. And use two tortillas on each of the longer sides of the pan. You should be able to cover all of the bottom and sides of the pan.

Let's start layering in the filling. Add the chutney into the bottom of the pan, on top of the tortillas, spreading it right to the edges. Now add half the mozzarella in an even layer.

In a separate bowl, mix the ground lamb with the yogurt and curry powder. Spread that onto the cheese in an even layer, again going right to the edges of the pan. Sprinkle with the red onion in an even layer.

Mix the paneer, garlic, and chile in another bowl. Now add this in an even layer on top of the onion. Add the poppadoms and really squash them in, then sprinkle with the cilantro and the rest of the cheese.

Add the last tortilla on top. Fold over the rest of the hanging tortillas and grease all over. Pop a piece of foil on top, along with a large baking sheet to weigh it down, and bake for 40 minutes.

Take out of the oven and let cool in the pan for 20 minutes. Turn out and cut into six portions. Get your mouth around that!

twice-baked squash

Serves 4–6	**Vegetarian**

1 large butternut squash

olive oil, for drizzling

4 cloves of garlic, minced

1 red onion, diced

½ cup/50g sliced almonds

2 teaspoons smoked paprika

salt

¼ cup/55g mayonnaise

To finish

3½ oz/100g smoked cheese, grated (1 cup)

½ cup/50g dried breadcrumbs

Simple dinners baked in the oven are my favorites, especially ones that can be eaten with just a fork. I do just a little of the work, while the oven does most of it. These squash halves get baked, the soft flesh is scooped out and mixed with other yummy things, then it's squashed back in and baked again. Enjoy dinner and the lack of washing-up, my friends.

Preheat the oven to 400°F.

Cut the squash in half lengthwise and spoon out the seeds from the cavity. Using a sharp knife, score the inside, getting as close to the bottom as possible without cutting all the way through. Drizzle generously with olive oil.

Now, fill the cavity with the garlic, onion, and almonds. Sprinkle with the paprika and salt.

Cover with foil and pop into the oven to bake for 1–1½ hours or until completely soft and cooked through. Take out of the oven and turn on the broiler to high.

Take the foil off and use a spoon to scrape the soft flesh into a bowl till all you have left is the squash peel. Mix the onion, garlic, and almonds into the squash flesh, then add the mayonnaise to the bowl and mix well. Spoon the mixture back into the butternut squash peel.

To finish, mix the grated cheese with the breadcrumbs, sprinkle over the butternut squash, and broil till golden. This is a perfect all-in-one dinner served straight out of the butternut squash.

stuffed squid

Serves 6

For the squid and filling

¾ cup/150g basmati rice, smashed

1 onion, finely diced

6 anchovy fillets, finely chopped

1 tablespoon capers, finely chopped

4 cloves of garlic, minced

2 teaspoons black pepper

1¾ lb/800g raw squid tubes, defrosted if frozen

For the sauce

oil, for drizzling

14 oz/400g cherry tomatoes

1 x 14-oz/400g can of diced tomatoes, plus half a can of water

2 tablespoons balsamic vinegar

1 tablespoon sugar

1 tablespoon chile flakes

To serve

chopped fresh basil

chopped fresh parsley

crusty bread

This is a delicious recipe of rice-stuffed squid that gently bakes in a sweet tomato sauce. Simple to make and easy to eat. Calamari isn't the only way to serve squid!

Start by making the squid filling. Place the smashed rice in a bowl, pour in enough boiling water to cover, and allow to stand for 20 minutes.

After 20 minutes, drain the rice and add the onion, anchovies, capers, garlic, and black pepper and mix well.

Have a few toothpicks ready to seal the squid. Stuff each tube with the rice mixture, leaving enough space for the rice to expand as it cooks. Use a toothpick to secure.

Preheat the oven to 400°F.

Get a roasting pan and drizzle in some oil. Add the cherry tomatoes, diced tomatoes (and extra water), balsamic, sugar, and chile and mix well. Add the stuffed squid tubes, cover with foil, and bake for 1 hour.

Halfway through cooking, flip the tubes, cover back up with the foil, and continue to cook. Take out and sprinkle with the fresh chopped herbs, and the dish is ready to be served.

kimchi chicken
with buttery miso leeks

Serves 4 Gluten-free

For the chicken

¼ cup/60g clarified butter (ghee)

¼ cup/75g white miso paste

a pinch of salt

4 large leeks, thinly sliced

3⅓ lb/1.5kg chicken, spatchcocked, with skin on

1⅓ cups/215g kimchi, roughly chopped

For the sticky rice

1½ cups/300g glutinous rice (Thai sticky rice)

2 cups/480ml cold water

1 tablespoon white vinegar

2 tablespoons dark soy sauce

1 tablespoon honey

Quite literally one of my favorite meals, this is packed with flavor, thanks to the kimchi on the chicken, the buttery miso leeks, and the sweet-and-sour drizzle that gets mixed into the sticky rice just before serving.

Preheat the oven to 400°F and have a large roasting pan ready.

Melt the clarified butter and mix in the miso to form a paste. Pour into the roasting pan. Add the sliced washed leeks with the salt and mix well. Make space in the center for the chicken to fit face down.

Now, take the chicken and gently tease your hands under the skin, starting at the breastbone and making sure to keep the skin intact. Once you have done that, spoon in the kimchi, pushing it all the way to the thighs and drumsticks. Once you have evenly distributed it, pop the chicken face-down in the center of the dish.

Cover with foil and bake for 30 minutes. Take the foil off and bake for another 30 minutes.

Meanwhile, make the rice. Combine the rice and the water in a nonstick pot and bring to a boil. Simmer with a lid on for 10–12 minutes. Turn off the heat and allow to steam for 5 minutes.

As soon as the chicken is out, finish off the rice by mixing the vinegar, soy, and honey, drizzling over the rice, and mixing in. Serve the rice alongside the kimchi chicken and buttery leeks.

pistachio and poppy seed cake

with pistachio praline

Serves 10	Vegetarian

For the cake

¾ cup plus 2 tablespoons/200g unsalted butter, softened

1 cup/200g granulated sugar

4 large eggs

1 cup plus 3 tablespoons/150g all-purpose flour, sifted

2½ teaspoons baking powder

¼ teaspoon salt

¾ cup/100g pistachios, blended to a crumb

⅓ cup/50g poppy seeds

3 tablespoons whole milk

For the praline

1¼ cups/250g granulated sugar

1 cup/150g pistachios

3 tablespoons poppy seeds

For the filling

½ cup plus 2 tablespoons/150g unsalted butter, very soft

5¼ oz/150g full-fat cream cheese, at room temperature

2½ cups/300g confectioners' sugar, sifted

1¼ cups/150g fresh raspberries

To decorate

fresh raspberries

pistachios

poppy seeds

A beautiful cake in two simple layers, this is a delicious, sweet bake with the vibrancy of pistachio, the crunch of poppy seeds, and the tart hit of raspberries. Pistachio is my favorite and here it's in the cake, the praline, and the filling; paired with poppy seeds, it's a delicious combination to rival any other cake.

Start by making the cake layers. Preheat the oven to 350°F. Grease and line two 8-inch/20cm cake pans.

Cream the butter and sugar together till light and fluffy. Add the eggs in, one by one, mixing after each addition. Add the flour, baking powder, salt, pistachios, poppy seeds, and milk and mix till you have a smooth batter. Divide the mixture between the two pans, level off, and bake for 25–30 minutes.

Meanwhile, make the praline. Put the sugar in a flat pan and set over medium heat. Have a baking sheet ready, lined with parchment paper. Keep heating the sugar till it is completely liquid. If you are using a thermometer, it needs to reach 248°F. →

As soon as the sugar is melted, add the nuts and poppy seeds and quickly mix them in, then immediately pour and flatten onto the sheet and let cool.

Take the cakes out of the oven and let cool in the pans for 5 minutes before turning out and allowing to cool completely on a cooling rack.

Make the filling by mixing the butter, cream cheese, and confectioners' sugar together. Break off 3½ oz/100g of the praline and blend to a smooth powder in a food processor, add to the filling, and mix well.

Now it's time to put the cake together. Pop one cake layer onto a serving plate. Add half the filling to the cake layer, then the raspberries. Arrange the other cake on top. Spread the rest of the filling on top of that and decorate with more raspberries, a sprinkle of crushed praline, extra pistachios, and some poppy seeds. Any leftover praline can be saved for a few days in an airtight container.

spiced cinnamon bun cake

Serves 6–8   Vegetarian

For the dough

2¾ cups/360g all-purpose flour, plus extra for dusting

2 x ¼-oz/7g packets of fast-acting dried yeast

½ cup/100g granulated sugar

5 tablespoons/75g unsalted butter, softened, plus extra for greasing

⅔ cup/160ml warm milk

1 large egg

For the filling

5 tablespoons/75g unsalted butter, softened

6 tablespoons/75g granulated sugar

2 teaspoons ground cinnamon

1 orange, finely grated zest only

For the glaze

½ cup plus 2 tablespoons/150g unsalted butter, very soft

5¼ oz/150g full-fat cream cheese, at room temperature

2½ cups/300g confectioners' sugar, sifted

2 teaspoons vanilla bean paste

If you like cinnamon buns, you will love this, because it's basically one large cinnamon bun that looks like it was made for the BFG! Once baked, it gets cut into wedges, with all the delicious, soft sweetness of a cinnamon swirly whirly—perfect for sharing.

Start by making the dough. Grease and line the bottom of a 9-inch/23cm round cake pan with a removable bottom or a regular cake pan.

Put the flour in a bowl with the yeast, sugar, and butter. Rub in the butter till completely incorporated. Make a well in the center and pour in the milk and egg. Bring the dough together and knead till you have an elastic, smooth dough. Put into a greased bowl, cover, and let rise to double in size.

Make the filling by putting the soft butter, sugar, cinnamon, and orange zest into a bowl and mixing it thoroughly.

Take the dough out of the bowl and roll out on a floured surface to a rectangle of 23 x 8 inches/ 60 x 20cm. Spread the filling mixture all over the dough and roll up from the longer edge. You now have a roll that is 23 inches/60cm long. Coil the dough gently into the pan, starting from the center and swirling it around itself. Make sure to leave some gaps in the swirl for the dough to grow.

Cover in greased plastic wrap and put in a warm place to rise. When the dough is almost done rising, preheat the oven to 375°F. As soon as the swirl of dough no longer has any gaps, take the covering off and bake in the oven for about 30 minutes. Take out and allow to cool in the pan completely.

Now make the glaze by mixing the butter, cream cheese, sugar, and vanilla together till you have a velvety smooth glaze. Spread all over the top of the cooled swirl. Take out of the pan, cut into wedges, and you will be seeing swirls for days.

neenish tart

Serves 6–8 **Vegetarian**

For the pastry
⅔ cup/85g all-purpose flour, plus extra for dusting
3 tablespoons almond flour
3 tablespoons confectioners' sugar
5 tablespoons/75g unsalted butter, chilled, cubed
1 large egg yolk
1–2 tablespoons cold water

For the cream filling
6 tablespoons/75g granulated sugar
3 large egg yolks
¼ cup/30g cornstarch
1½ cups plus 1 tablespoon/375ml heavy cream
2 teaspoons vanilla bean paste
6 tablespoons/125g raspberry jam

For the icing
1⅔ cups/200g fondant icing sugar
1 tablespoon water
2 tablespoons milk
2 teaspoons cocoa powder
pink gel food coloring

With this recipe, Australia proves it has more to give us than koalas and lamingtons; now it also gives us neenish tart. I love sweet desserts, and this is just that, with its buttery pastry, tangy jam, sweet cream, and an even sweeter icing. Apart from baking neenish, I also just really like saying the word *neenish*!

Start by making the pastry. Put the flour in a food processor with the almond flour, confectioners' sugar, and butter and whiz to a breadcrumb-like texture. Add the egg yolk and water and blend the mixture to a clump of dough. Take the dough ball and pop onto a well-floured surface.

Roll out the dough and use it to line the inside of a 9-inch/23cm round fluted tart pan. Line so there is a little bit of overhang. Prick the base with a fork and pop into the fridge.

Preheat the oven to 375°F.

Take the pastry case out of the fridge and line with parchment paper. Add some baking beads and blind bake for 15 minutes. Take out, remove the paper and baking beads, and bake the pastry for 10 minutes.

Take out and trim off the edges after 5 minutes, while still warm.

Now make the cream filling by putting the granulated sugar, egg yolks, cornstarch, cream, and vanilla in a small nonstick pot. Pop onto medium heat and whisk continuously till the mixture is really thick. Pour out of the pot into a bowl, cover with plastic wrap, and set aside to cool. After 15 minutes, place in the fridge to chill completely.

Spoon the jam into the bottom of the tart shell and spread in an even layer. Add the chilled cream filling and spread into an even layer. Pop into the fridge.

Make the icing by putting the fondant icing sugar, water, and milk in a bowl and mixing to a smooth paste. Divide the mixture equally into two small bowls and add cocoa to one and pink food coloring to the other. Mix well and you should have two vibrant colors.

Take the tart out and pour the icing over the top from either side till both colors meet in the middle. Where the two colors meet, use a skewer to swirl the colors together.

Refrigerate for 1 hour and you are ready to slice and eat this sweet, colorful beauty.

monkey bubble bread

Serves 12   Vegetarian

For the bread balls

2¾ cups/360g white bread flour

1 x ¼-oz/7g packet of fast-acting dried yeast

3 tablespoons granulated sugar

¼ cup/55g unsalted butter, softened, plus extra for greasing

⅔ cup/160ml whole milk

1 large egg, lightly beaten

40–45 chocolate malt balls

5 tablespoons/75g unsalted butter, melted

½ cup/100g granulated sugar

For the glaze

¾ cup/100g confectioners' sugar

1 tablespoon milk

1 tablespoon unsalted butter

a pinch of salt

½ teaspoon vanilla extract

crushed chocolate malt balls, for decorating

Bread-baking fun is right where it is at with this recipe. Assembled from 40 small balls of dough, each filled with a crisp chocolate malt ball, baked together, and covered in sticky syrup, it's the ultimate bake for a sharing treat or dessert. You'll find more pictures on the next page.

Start by making the dough. Put the flour in a bowl with the yeast, sugar, and butter. Rub in the butter till any large lumps have completely disappeared.

Make a well in the center of the mixture and add the milk and egg. Mix till you have a dough. Knead in a stand mixer with a dough hook on high for 6 minutes, until the dough is elastic and smooth. Pop into a greased bowl, cover, and let rise till doubled in size. As soon as it has, uncover the bowl, tip out the dough and flatten.

Grease a 10-inch/25cm Bundt pan with butter. Shape the dough into 40 equal-size balls. If you have a bit more dough left, a few extra balls are fine. Have your chocolate malt balls ready, along with the melted butter and sugar for coating.

Take a dough ball and flatten. Add a malt ball into the center and encase in the dough. Dip into the melted butter and then into the sugar and drop into the pan. Do this till you have piled all the balls into the pan. Cover with greased plastic wrap and let rise in a warm place for 20 minutes.

Preheat the oven to 350°F.

Take off the plastic wrap and bake for 35 minutes. Once baked, let cool in the pan for at least 15 minutes before turning out onto a plate.

Meanwhile, make the glaze. Put the confectioners' sugar, milk, butter, salt, and vanilla in a small pot and slowly heat till the mixture is smooth. Let cool for 10 minutes or until thickened a little.

Drizzle the glaze all over the bread, sprinkle with the crushed chocolate malt balls, and you are ready to serve. To eat, slice up or simply pinch off little balls of sweet, malty, doughy deliciousness!   →

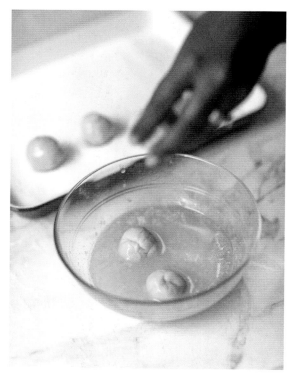 

chapter six
OUTDOOR DAYS

granola breakfast cups

Makes 12   Vegetarian/Gluten-free

As a family, we spend a lot of time walking in the woods, exploring and hiking, and in general getting tired and mucky. But our conversations always begin with "what will we eat?" These breakfast granola cups are what we take for early starts: sweet, chewy little granola vessels that make the perfect vehicle for all sorts of other yummy things. We like to fill ours with yogurt, berries, and—if we're feeling fancy—some edible herbs and flowers from the garden.

Preheat the oven to 350°F and have a 12-hole cupcake pan ready and very lightly greased.

Put the butter, sugar, and golden syrup in a pot and heat till the butter has melted. Pour the mixture into a bowl and add the oats, sunflower seeds, nuts, cinnamon, and berries. Mix really well till everything is combined.

For the granola cups

7 tablespoons/100g unsalted butter, plus extra for greasing

packed ½ cup/100g brown sugar

3 tablespoons golden syrup or light corn syrup

2¼ cups/200g rolled oats

¾ cup/100g sunflower seeds

¾ cup/100g chopped nuts

1 teaspoon ground cinnamon

1 cup/100g dried berries, chopped

3½ oz/100g dark chocolate, melted

To serve

yogurt

fruit

fresh herbs

edible flowers

Divide the mixture among the 12 holes till you have used it all up. Now use the end of a rolling pin to push a hole into the granola mix, making sure the granola is always tightly packed in and not loose. Do this to all 12. Pop into the oven and bake for 20–25 minutes.

As soon as the cups come out of the oven, and while they are still warm, use the end of the rolling pin again to make sure you still have a well-defined hole in the middle of each cup. Let cool completely in the pan.

Melt the chocolate in the microwave, then use a pastry brush to brush the insides of the cups generously with chocolate. This will not only strengthen the cups but also create a waterproof barrier to prevent our cups from getting soggy when we add the yogurt.

Fill the cups with yogurt and decorate with your choice of fruit, herbs, and flowers to serve. Yummy and simple.

cheat's almond croissant rolls

Makes 12   Vegetarian

I like nothing more on a morning than a sweet almond croissant with a caffeinated beverage. But while I do love making croissants from scratch, I don't always have the time or energy so if, like me, you are in the "not always" gang, then these are for you. They are almost as easy to make as they would be to buy, using ready-to-bake croissant dough and a sweet almond butter filling. They're topped with toasted almonds and—the best bit—copious amounts of dusted confectioners' sugar.

Start by making the filling. Put the almond flour, butter, granulated sugar, and almond extract in a bowl and mix into a really thick paste.

Preheat the oven to 400°F and lightly grease and line two baking sheets or roasting pans.

For the filling

1½ cups/150g almond flour

7 tablespoons/100g unsalted butter, melted, plus extra for greasing

6 tablespoons/75g granulated sugar

1½ teaspoons almond extract

2 packages of ready-to-bake croissant dough

For the topping

1 egg, lightly beaten

1 cup/100g sliced almonds

confectioners' sugar

Open one package of the croissant dough and unroll onto a lightly floured surface. You will see when you open it up that there are perforated triangles—ignore them and keep the dough as it is. Take half the filling and spread all over. Roll up, starting from the short end.

Now, do the same with the other package of dough and the remaining filling. Cut each roll into 6 slices. This will create a total of 12 rolls.

Place each one swirl-side down on the prepared baking sheets, with about 1 inch/2.5cm space between them so they have room to grow as they bake. Brush each roll with egg wash and sprinkle with the sliced almonds, pressing them on. Bake for 15 minutes.

Once they are out, allow them to cool on the sheets and really dust them with the confectioners' sugar, being very generous. It's not a proper almond croissant if you're not covered in confectioners' sugar and toasted nuts. I love eating these while they are still warm, alongside my morning tea.

cheese and onion Welsh cakes

Makes 24   Vegetarian

1¾ cups plus 1 tablespoons/225g all-purpose flour, plus extra for dusting

½ teaspoon baking powder

1 teaspoon onion granules

1 teaspoon onion seeds

2 teaspoons dried chives

7 tablespoons/100g unsalted butter, diced, plus extra for greasing

1¾ oz/50g semi-firm cheese, finely grated, plus extra for the top

1 large egg, beaten

2 tablespoons cold whole milk

To my purist friends out there: don't shout at me, please! I love making these, just as I also love making a million other variations. With their cheese and onion flavor, these mini Welsh cakes are savory instead of sweet, and baked instead of griddled, so they are definitely not traditional, but I promise you the changes are worth making.

Start by putting the flour in a bowl along with the baking powder, onion granules, seeds, and dried chives and mix so everything is evenly dispersed. Add the butter and rub in using your fingertips till there are no large lumps and the mixture resembles breadcrumbs.

Mix in the cheese and then make a well in the center. Add the egg and milk and mix it all in, bringing the dough together. Be careful not to knead the mixture or the Welsh cakes will become tough.

Preheat the oven to 375°F and have a baking sheet at the ready, very lightly greased—just enough to prevent anything from sticking.

Roll out the dough on a lightly floured surface to a thickness of about ¼ inch/½cm. Using a 1½-inch/4cm fluted cutter, cut out rounds and pop onto the sheet. Do this till you have used up all the dough.

Bake for 10 minutes, then take out, turn each cake, sprinkle each one with cheese, and bake for 5 minutes.

Let cool completely and then they are ready to eat or pack away as a perfect traveling picnic companion.

orange semolina cake

For the cake

1¼ cups/200g fine semolina

¼ cup/25g dried shredded coconut

⅓ cup/40g all-purpose flour

¾ cup plus 2 tablespoons 175g granulated sugar

⅓ cup/80ml olive oil, plus extra for greasing

7 tablespoons/125g Greek yogurt

¾ cup/180ml whole milk

2 teaspoons orange blossom water

2 teaspoons baking powder

½ teaspoon baking soda

For the syrup

juice of 1 lime

juice of 1 lemon

¼ cup/50g granulated sugar

⅓ cup/80ml water

1 large orange

Makes 9 squares   **Vegetarian**

My mum doesn't much like cake, but she loves semolina, so this is one cake that I make for her all the time. The semolina makes it dense and is the perfect vehicle for the sweet orange blossom syrup that it drinks up when hot and baked. This cake is simple, sweet, and perfect for when you are out and about.

Lightly grease and line an 8-inch/20cm square pan, ideally with a removable bottom if you have one.

Start by putting all the dry cake ingredients in a bowl: the semolina, coconut, flour, and sugar. Mix well.

Now, pour the oil, yogurt, milk, and orange blossom water into the dry ingredients and mix till you have an even cake batter. Let rest, covered, for about 40 minutes to allow the semolina and coconut to soak up that liquid.

Preheat the oven to 375°F.

Uncover the bowl, add the baking powder and baking soda, and mix in well. Spoon the mixture into the prepared cake pan and spread into a thin, even layer. Bake for 35 minutes, till a skewer comes out clean.

While the cake is baking, make the syrup. Squeeze the juice of the lime and lemon into a small pot and add the sugar and the water. Slice the orange into thin slices and add to the syrup mixture. Pop onto the heat, bring to a boil, and let simmer on the lowest heat for 20 minutes.

As soon as the cake is out of the oven, poke holes all over with a skewer. Slowly drizzle the syrup right onto the hot cake. Spread the slices of orange all over.

Let cool in the pan for 30 minutes. Take out, slice, and this sweet, zesty semolina cake is ready to eat.

lamb samosa balls

Makes 15

For the filling

2 tablespoons oil

1 lb/450g ground lamb

1 teaspoon garlic paste

1½ teaspoons salt

3 tablespoons garam masala

⅓ cup/50g frozen peas

1 red onion, finely diced

2 small green chiles, thinly sliced

a small handful of fresh cilantro

For the coating

15 slices of white bread, crusts removed

4 large eggs, lightly beaten

a pinch of salt

½ teaspoon ground turmeric

2 cups/200g dried breadcrumbs

cooking oil spray

If you know me, then you will know how much I love a samosa! They are my go-to for celebrations, for life, for every day in general. I find all sorts of ways to make them. Of course, I love the traditional triangle, but this recipe is a riff on all the good things that come with a samosa. Same spicy filling, same crisp coating but in the form of a baked ball.

Start by making the filling. Pour the oil into a frying pan and heat. As soon as the oil is hot, add the lamb, cook, and break up till the meat has browned.

Now add the garlic, salt, garam masala, and peas. Cook till the peas are no longer frozen and the liquid has completely evaporated.

Take off the heat and transfer to a bowl to cool. As soon as the mixture is cool, add the fresh ingredients of onion, chile, and cilanatro and mix well.

Have a plate or baking sheet ready that will comfortably fit in your freezer.

Put some water on a small plate. Take each slice of bread, quickly dunk one side and then squeeze the water out, really flattening the piece of bread.

Now, add a generous amount of the filling into the center and wrap the whole thing around. If there is too much filling, take some out; if there isn't enough, add some more. Shape into a ball and really pinch the seams. Do this to all of the slices of bread and pop onto the plate and straight into the freezer for 1 hour.

After 1 hour, heat the oven to 375°F. Have a baking sheet ready.

Mix the eggs with the salt and turmeric and whisk to combine. Have the breadcrumbs ready on a flat plate.

Dip a ball into the egg and then the breadcrumbs. Do the same to the other 14 balls. Now do it all over again. Double coating will not only make them crispy but will also prevent the filling from falling out.

Spray each of the balls generously with oil and bake in the oven for 25–30 minutes, till crisp and golden. I love eating these with ketchup. They need nothing else!

pineapple and chile-marinated lamb ribs

| Serves 4 | Gluten-free |

For the lamb ribs

1 x 8-oz 227g can of pineapple in juice

1 teaspoon salt

1 tablespoon vinegar

6 green chiles

4 cloves of garlic

a large handful of fresh cilantro

2 lb 2 oz/1kg lamb ribs

oil, for roasting

For the corn riblets

4 large corn on the cob

oil, for roasting

a large pinch of salt

2 tablespoons paprika

Pineapple has these magical enzymes that help to break down and tenderize meats and I am down for that. I still can't get my head around pineapple on pizza, but this recipe I can do, with sweet-and-spicy pineapple-marinated lamb ribs, cooked to perfection and served with paprika corn riblets. And if we're getting our hands in, then we're really getting our hands in!

Start by making the marinade. Put the pineapple, salt, vinegar, chiles, garlic, and cilantro in a food processor. Blend till you have a smooth paste.

Put the ribs in a dish, pour in the marinade, and chill in the fridge overnight to marinate.

Take out of the fridge and remove the ribs from the marinade, saving the marinade. Preheat the oven to 400°F. Pour some oil into a roasting pan, add the ribs, and cover with foil.

To prepare the corn, cut the cobs in half so you have eight short pieces. With the flat end on a board, steady the corn and cut right the way down so it is halved. Now, lay on the flat edge and cut into quarters. Do this to all of the corn. Use a sharp knife and be very careful, as the corn can be tricky to cut.

Put the strips of corn quarters in another roasting pan, drizzle with the oil, sprinkle on salt and paprika, and massage into the corn, then cover with foil. Pop both dishes into the oven with the lamb on top and corn underneath.

Meanwhile, add a little oil to a frying pan, pour in the marinade mix, and cook gently till the marinade is thick.

After 30 minutes in the oven, remove the foil from both dishes. Pour the thickened sauce onto the ribs and turn the corn. Pop back into the oven for 20 minutes to get some more color on them. Now they are ready to eat. Time to get your fingers in!

beet salad with crispy chile crabsticks

1 lb 7 oz/660g fresh beets (ideally a mix of colors)

oil, for roasting

salt and ground black pepper

For the crispy crabsticks

4¼ oz/120g crabsticks (imitation crab), shredded

oil, for drizzling

2 tablespoons all-purpose flour

1 teaspoon chile powder

1 teaspoon salt

For the dressing

½ cup/100g sour cream

1 oz/30g fresh chives, finely chopped

2 cloves of garlic, minced

1 tablespoon honey

3 tablespoons milk

Serves 4

I openly admit to not being a massive fan of salads unless they are out-of-this-world delicious, and this salad is *way-out-of-this-world delicious*. Sweet, simply roasted beets are served warm with garlic and chive sour cream and topped off with crispy crabsticks. I like to use a few different varieties of beet for a mix of colors.

Preheat the oven to 400°F.

Start by preparing the beet. Peel and quarter the beets and put in a roasting pan with some oil. Season well and pop into the oven for 30 minutes.

Spread the shredded crabsticks onto a baking sheet and drizzle with oil to cover them.

Mix the flour with the chile and salt. Sprinkle the mixture over the crabsticks to cover them evenly, mixing well so all the oil and flour coat the crabsticks. Pop into the oven to crisp up for 12 to 15 minutes.

Make the dressing by mixing together the sour cream, chives, garlic, honey, and milk.

Take the beet and crabsticks out of the oven and transfer both to a serving dish.

Drizzle the sour cream dressing over the top, and get ready to crunch on those crabsticks. Hello, yummy warm salad. Goodbye, cold not very yummy salad.

plantain subs
with quick pickles

Makes 4 Vegetarian

For the subs

oil, for drizzling

2 large yellow plantains

salt and pepper

¾ cup/180g mayo

3 tablespoons jerk paste

4 crispy baguettes,
  sliced lengthwise

fresh cilantro

For the quick pickles

2 carrots, peeled and
  sliced into thin ribbons

1 red onion, thinly sliced

½ cucumber, sliced into
  ribbons

1⅔ cups/400ml apple
  cider vinegar

5 tablespoons/60g
  sugar

Subs are my go-to when feeding my lot, and I love seeing their reaction when I make them with something a bit interesting. This is one of my kids' absolute favorites: crispy discs of seasoned plantain, packed into a crunchy baguette with spicy mayo and quick-pickled veg.

Preheat the oven to 400°F.

Peel and slice the plantains into ½-inch/1cm coins.

Drizzle two large baking sheets with oil. Add the plantain coins to the sheets and mix to coat in the oil. Season and arrange in a single layer, then pop into the oven for 20 minutes.

Meanwhile, make the pickle. Have the veg ready, then put the vinegar and sugar in a medium pot and bring to a boil. Add the carrot, onion, and cucumber. Bring to a boil and then let simmer for 15 minutes. Drain and set aside.

Take the plantain out of the oven and, using the bottom of a flat glass, squash the plantain to create ridges that will bake and get crispier. Pop back in for 10 minutes.

Meanwhile, mix the mayo with the jerk paste. Spread onto the inside of the baguettes liberally. Lay cilantro into each baguette. Take the plantain out of the oven and layer generously on top of the cilantro. Finally, add the pickles.

Give each baguette a squeeze and you are ready to get your teeth around your sub!

achari chicken pie

Serves 8–10

For the filling

5 tablespoons/75ml olive oil

3 onions, finely diced

1½ teaspoons salt

1 tablespoon ginger paste

1 tablespoon garlic paste

2 tablespoons dried chile flakes

5 heaped tablespoons mango lime pickle

1 lb 2 oz/500g chicken thighs, chopped into ½-inch/1cm chunks

1⅓ cups/200g frozen peas

1 lb 2 oz/500g potatoes, peeled, diced, boiled, and drained

finely chopped fresh cilantro

For the pastry

½ cup plus 2 tablespoons/140ml boiling water

⅓ cup/65g vegetable shortening

2 cups plus 2 tablespoons/265g all-purpose flour

½ cup/55g white bread flour

2 tablespoons cayenne pepper

1 egg, beaten, for brushing

Pies, pies, I love pies! Simple or complicated; hot or cold; made or bought; handheld or with cutlery—whichever way it comes, I love a pie! This achari pie is a thing of beauty with its tender chicken thighs cooked in spices and flavorful mixed pickle, all bound in a robust spiced cayenne pastry.

Start by making the filling. Pour the oil into a large pot and heat. As soon as the oil is hot, add the onion, salt, ginger, garlic, and chile flakes and cook till the onion is soft.

Add the mixed pickle and the chicken thighs and cook on high heat till any liquid in the pot is absorbed fully. Add the peas and warm them through.

Mash the potato using the back of a fork and add to the chicken mix. Once you've mixed it in, you should have a mixture that really holds it shape. Take off the heat, add the cilantro, and mix well. Let cool.

Now, make the pastry by pouring the hot water into a medium nonstick pan with the shortening. As soon as the water has come to a boil and the shortening has melted, take off the heat.

Mix the flours and cayenne pepper together well and then add to the water mix. Stir fast till you have a dough that comes together.

Preheat the oven to 400°F. Very lightly grease an 8-inch/20cm round pan with a removable bottom.

Take two-thirds of the pastry and roll out on a lightly floured surface to a size that's large enough to line the bottom and sides of the pan. Once the pan is lined, add the filling into the pastry case. Level off the top.

Roll out the smaller piece of pastry so that it's large enough to cover the pie. Use beaten egg to brush the edges of the pastry that's already in the pan. Add the pastry lid. Trim and crimp the edges. Chill in the fridge for 30 minutes.

Glaze the top of the pie with beaten egg, cut a steam hole in the center, and bake in the oven for 1 hour. Once out of the oven, let cool in the pan before taking out. Ideally chill this beauty and cut into large wedges for eating.

nutty tuna cake

Serves 6–8

3 tablespoons oil, plus extra for greasing

3 cloves of garlic, minced

1 teaspoon salt

2 teaspoons ground black pepper

1 onion, diced

1 large red bell pepper, diced

1 large carrot, grated

7 oz/200g mushrooms, diced

2 x 5-oz/145g cans of tuna, drained

2 tablespoons tomato paste

2 tablespoons smoked paprika

1¼ cups/300ml vegetable stock

1 cup/100g dried breadcrumbs

1⅓ cups/150g chopped nuts

3 large eggs

5¼ oz/150g mature cheddar cheese, grated (1⅓ cups)

a large handful of fresh parsley

Lots of vegetables, nuts, and tuna create this baked savory loaf that is great eaten for lunch. And it is the gift that keeps on giving, as it's even better the day after it's made. I love it sliced up and served inside a heavily buttered bun.

Start by pouring the oil into a pot. As soon as the oil is hot, add the garlic, salt, and pepper and cook till brown. Add the onion, red bell pepper, carrot, and mushrooms and cook for 10 minutes, till softened.

Now, add the tuna, tomato, paprika, and vegetable stock and really turn the heat up. Cook till the mixture has thickened and the liquid completely evaporated. Pop into a bowl and let cool completely.

Preheat the oven to 375°F and lightly grease and line a 9 x 5-inch/900g loaf pan.

When the mixture is cool, add the breadcrumbs, nuts, eggs, and cheese and mix.

Spoon the mixture into the pan and level off. Cover with foil and bake for 30 minutes. After 30 minutes, take off the foil and bake for 20 minutes.

Take out of the oven and let cool in the pan completely. This will help to firm up the cake and make it easier to slice. Cut into slices and eat with a simple salad. Or do like me and take a huge slice of the tuna cake with that salad and wedge them both right inside a generously buttered floury bun.

cake in a jar

For the cake

½ cup/125g unsalted butter, softened

½ cup plus 2 tablespoons/ 125g granulated sugar

2 large eggs

1 cup/125g all-purpose flour, sifted

1½ teaspoons baking powder

¼ teaspoon salt

6 tablespoons/80g rainbow sprinkles

2½ oz/75g popping candy

For the jelly

1 x 3 oz/85g package of strawberry jell-o

2 cups/480ml boiling water

10½ oz/300g strawberries, cubed

For the frosting

7 tablespoons/100g unsalted butter, very soft

3½ oz/100g cream cheese, at room temperature

1⅔ cups/200g confectioners' sugar, sifted

6 tablespoons/80g rainbow sprinkles

Makes 6 × 15-oz/445ml jars   Vegetarian

This fun recipe can be adapted to use any cake you want, whether homemade, leftover, or store-bought. Because the rest of the recipe is so easy, I personally love to make the cake from scratch, adding sprinkles for extra color. The cake gets crumbled and layered up with a smooth cream cheese frosting (with more sprinkles!), a fruity strawberry jelly, and a surprise hit of popping candy for even more fun. Built straight into a jam jar, these are perfectly transportable for picnics or just for when you're sitting in the garden.

Start by baking the cake. Preheat the oven to 350°F. Grease and line an 8-inch/20cm round cake pan.

Put the butter, sugar, eggs, flour, baking powder, and salt in a bowl and beat for 3 minutes till you have a mixture that is smooth and shiny. Now, add the sprinkles and fold them in. Spoon into the pan, level off, and bake for 30–35 minutes.

→

While the cake bakes, let's make the jelly. We want a firm set jelly that really holds. For 3 oz/85g of jell-o, I recommend making it with 2 cups/480ml of hot water, which is a little less than the amount of water normally advised on the package. Put the jell-o in a dish, pour in the water, and stir till there are no crystals left. Allow to set in the fridge.

Make the frosting by whisking the butter and cream cheese together till totally combined and there are no streaks of butter left. Add the confectioners' sugar and combine well until thick. Add the sprinkles, fold them in, and then transfer the frosting to a piping bag.

Once the cake is done, let cool in the pan for 10 minutes. Remove from the pan and let cool completely on a cooling rack.

Now we have all our elements ready: cooled cake, set jelly, strawberries, and frosting. Line up the jars and take off the lids. Crumble up your cooled cake into pieces and drop an even layer into each jar. Sprinkle with the popping candy. Pipe in a layer of frosting right on top. Do this to all six.

Use a fork to break up the jelly. Mix in the cubes of strawberry. Add a layer of the strawberry jelly into each jar. Now, repeat the layers (cake, popping candy, frosting, jelly), till you run out of ingredients or space in the jars. Pop the lids on and you can pack these away in the fridge till you are ready to eat.

caramel pecan pie

Serves 8   Vegetarian

For the pastry

2 cups plus 6 tablespoons/300g all-purpose flour, plus extra for dusting

½ cup plus 2 tablespoons/125g granulated sugar ¾ cup/175g unsalted butter, cubed

1 teaspoon vanilla powder

1 large egg

a pinch of salt

beaten egg, to finish

For the filling

packed 1 cup plus 3 tablespoons/250g brown sugar

2 tablespoons golden syrup or light corn syrup

¾ cup plus 2 tablespoons/200ml heavy cream

3 cups/300g pecans, thinly sliced

1 orange, finely grated zest only

½ teaspoon salt

I like very sweet desserts, especially pecan pie, but sometimes I find the sheer sweetness means the whole thing could do with a bit more pastry. So, in this recipe that's exactly what I've added: it is like a pecan pie, but with a top, and the pastry is less like pastry and more like buttery shortbread. Baked and chilled, it's sweet, buttery, and crunchy, with a hint of orange that really hits the spot.

Start by making the pastry. Put the flour, sugar, butter, and vanilla in a food processor and blitz till you have no more lumps of butter. Now, drop in the egg and salt and whiz just till you have a smooth dough.

Separate the dough into two-thirds and one-third. Flatten both pieces into a flat round shape, wrap each piece in plastic wrap, and chill in the fridge for 30 minutes.

Lightly grease a 9-inch/23cm tart pan.

Take out the larger dough piece and on a lightly floured surface roll out the pastry to cover the bottom and sides of the pan, leaving a little overhang where you can attach the lid. Now, roll out the smaller dough piece until large enough to fit the top of the pan as a lid, ensuring there is some overhang. Keep the lid separate for now.

Chill both the tart case and the lid in the fridge while you make the caramel.

Put the sugar and golden syrup into a large flat pan and shake till the sugar is in an even layer. Turn the heat to medium and allow the sugar to melt gently from the outside in. Watch it. Don't walk away. Slowly the sugar should melt till totally liquid.

As soon as the sugar has melted, turn the heat down and add the cream. It will start to bubble away, and then turn the heat right up and allow the mixture to bubble and thicken. Take off the heat and add the pecans, orange zest, and salt and mix well. Let cool completely.

Take the tart case out of the fridge. Fill with the pecan filling and spread into an even layer. Brush the top edge of the tart case with beaten egg and add the lid on top. Make a small slit in the top. Trim the edges and crimp. Chill in the freezer for at least 30 minutes.

Preheat the oven to 400°F.

Brush the top of the chilled tart with beaten egg. Bake in the oven for 25–30 minutes.

Take out and let cool completely. Chill for at least 3 hours and then you are ready to eat a sweet, decadent slice.

chocolate bombe

Serves 8–10	**Vegetarian**

For the cake

oil, for greasing

6 large eggs

1 cup/200g sugar

1 cup/130g all-
purpose flour, sifted

1½ teaspoons baking
powder

¼ teaspoon salt

6 tablespoons/35g
cocoa powder, sifted

For the filling

2½ cups/213g
marshmallow fluff

For the ice cream

1 quart/1 liter
chocolate ice cream

1 quart/1 liter vanilla
ice cream

1 x 5.5-oz/154g
package of
sandwiched
chocolate and
vanilla cookies,
cookie and filling
separated

This old classic can be done again and again, and I would never get bored. So, let's make it! Here I've gone for stripes instead of swirls, with cocoa-laced cake, marshmallow fluff, and a two-tone ice cream filling.

Start by making the cake. Preheat the oven to 400°F. Grease and line two 9 x 13-inch/23 x 33cm pans..

Put the eggs and sugar in a bowl and whisk the mixture till it is thick and fluffy and doubled in size. Mix the flour, baking powder, salt, and cocoa and add to the egg mixture, being sure to fold in gently to make sure you keep as much of that air in as possible.

Divide the mixture between the two pans, leveling off the top. Bake for 10–12 minutes, till the cake is firm on top.

Take out and let cool in the pans for 5 minutes. Tip out onto some parchment paper, peel off the paper you lined the pans with, and let cool completely.

Take both ice creams out of the freezer to allow them to soften a little.

Warm the marshmallow fluff in the microwave for 15 seconds on high or until spreadable. Spread it onto one of the cake layers. Take the other cake and place right on top.

Grease a glass bowl with an 8-inch/20cm diameter (about 4 inches/10cm deep) and line the inside with plastic wrap. Cut ½-inch/1cm strips of the sandwiched cake and use to line the inside of the bowl in strips so you can see the marshmallow exposed. I like to do this in stripes (instead of the swirls you usually see on a chocolate bombe). I start each strip from the middle of the bowl and work my way around the bowl, arranging the cake in straight lines radiating from the center out. You should have about a third of the cake left to use later. Try to fill in all the holes using any offcuts. Cover the bowl and place in the freezer.

Now, take the softened ice creams. Add the vanilla filling of the cookies to the chocolate ice cream and mix. Crumble the chocolate cookies into the vanilla ice cream and mix. Dollop the ice cream into the bombe, alternating each type.

Take the leftover cake and arrange it on top of the ice cream to completely enclose. Cover with plastic wrap and allow to set in the freezer for at least 2 hours. When you take it out, let it thaw out for half an hour before slicing and enjoying.

meringue pops

3 large egg whites

1¼ cups/250g sugar

gel food coloring

6 long lollipop sticks

dried flowers/sprinkles,
    to decorate

5¼ oz/150g white
    chocolate, melted

⅓ oz/9g freeze-dried
    raspberries

Makes 6   Vegetarian/Gluten-free

These are so much fun to make, not to mention delicious and beautiful. Crisp on the outside and chewy on the inside, simple meringue is baked onto sticks and sandwiched with chocolate for an alternative to a lollipop and a great treat for children and grown-ups alike. They are lovely wrapped up as a gift or also look amazing as cake toppers.

Start by lining two baking sheets with parchment paper. Preheat the oven to 200°F.

Take a bowl and wipe with some vinegar to remove any grease. Pour in the egg whites and start whisking. As soon as they begin to get frothy, add a small spoonful of sugar, one at a time, till the sugar is incorporated after each addition. Keep going till you have used up all the sugar. You should have a mixture that is stiff and glossy.

Take a paintbrush and dip it into the food coloring. Paint a generous line of coloring all the way up the inside of a piping bag. Now, add the meringue straight in. The painted line will create a beautiful streak of color as you pipe.

Place a lollipop stick flat on the sheet so you have enough room to pipe right on top of it. Pipe a swirl of meringue onto one end of the stick, starting in the center and piping all the way around several times to create a circle. Pipe another swirl of meringue right next to it, the exact same size, but without a stick—this is the one to be sandwiched later. Do this till you have filled the sheets with six meringue swirls with sticks underneath and six without.

Sprinkle with the dried flowers or sprinkles and bake for 1 hour. After 1 hour, turn the oven off, open the oven door, and let cool completely.

Now, take the melted chocolate, mix in the freeze-dried berries, and use this as the glue to sandwich the meringues together. Do this to all six. Once the chocolate has set, they are ready to wrap as gifts or eat as a treat.

chapter seven
CELEBRATION DAYS

breakfast pizza

Makes 2 × 12-inch/30cm pizzas

For the dough

3¼ cups/400g white bread flour, plus extra for dusting

1 x ¼-oz/7g package of fast-acting dried yeast

1 teaspoon salt

1 teaspoon sugar

2 tablespoons oil, plus extra for greasing

¾ cup plus 3 tablespoons/225ml water

For the topping

5 tablespoons/85g ketchup

5 tablespoons/90g steak sauce

¾ cup/200g baked beans

1 cup/100g shredded mozzarella

a small handful of mushrooms, sliced

4 cooked breakfast sausages, sliced

crispy fried onions

2 large eggs

My kids like celebration pizzas, so no matter what we're celebrating, we have a pizza for it! We even have a breakfast pizza with all the things we love in the morning but on a pizza crust. Here it is: soft dough, tomato and bean sauce, mushrooms, sausage, and eggs to celebrate the day ahead!

Start by making the dough. Combine the flour, yeast, salt, and sugar and mix really well. Add the oil and mix in. Make a well in the center and pour in the water. Bring the dough together. Now, knead the dough till you have dough that is stretchy and smooth.

Grease a large bowl very lightly with oil, put in the dough, cover, and let rise in a warm place to double in size.

Preheat the oven to 425°F. Have two baking sheets ready and the toppings for your pizza.

Divide the dough into two equal balls and roll each one out to a 12-inch/30cm circle, making sure to create a raised rim around the edge. Pop onto the two sheets.

Mix the ketchup, steak sauce, and beans and spread over the dough. Sprinkle with the cheese. Add the sliced mushrooms, sliced sausages, and crispy onions.

Crack 1 egg into the center of each pizza and bake in the oven for 15 minutes. There you have it: breakfast pizza.

→

plum half-moons

Makes 10   Vegetarian

For the pastry

2 cups/250g all-purpose flour

½ teaspoon salt

½ cup/125g unsalted butter

6 tablespoons/90ml cold water

salt

For the filling

5 oz/145g plums, thinly sliced

6 tablespoons/75g granulated sugar

½ cup/50g granola

½ teaspoon ground cinnamon

½ teaspoon ground ginger

½ teaspoon nutmeg

1 tablespoon cornstarch

1 egg, lightly beaten

confectioners' sugar, for dusting (optional)

Breakfast is best when all you need are your hands; it generally means more fun and less washing-up. These half-moons are made with buttery pastry and filled with a lightly spiced mixture of sliced plums and granola, for a different way to start the day.

Start by making the pastry. Put the flour in a food processer with the salt and butter and blitz till there are no longer lumps of butter. Add the water and blitz till you have a clump of dough. Bring the dough together, wrap in plastic wrap and chill in the fridge for 30 minutes.

Preheat the oven to 400°F and line two baking sheets with parchment paper.

Make the filling by putting the plums in a bowl with the sugar, granola, cinnamon, ginger, nutmeg, and cornstarch and mix well.

Take out the pastry and roll out to ⅛-inch/3mm thick. Cut out ten 4-inch/10cm circles. Take one circle and add filling to one half. Brush a little beaten egg around the edge of the pastry. Fold the pastry over to cover the filling, creating the half-moon. Crimp to seal, using the back of a fork. Place onto the baking sheet.

Do this to all the pastries, then brush them all with beaten egg and chill for 20 minutes.

Pierce the top of each pie to allow steam out. Sprinkle with some salt and bake for 25 minutes. As soon as they are out, dust with confectioners' sugar, if you like, and they are ready to eat.

pretzel bites with cheese sauce

For the pretzels

4 cups/500g white bread flour

1 x ¼-oz/7g package of fast-acting dried yeast

2 tablespoons sugar

¼ cup/50g unsalted butter, softened

1–1¼ cups/240–300ml water

oil, for greasing

3 tablespoons baking soda

1 egg, lightly beaten

flaky salt

For the cheese sauce

2 tablespoons unsalted butter

2 tablespoons all-purpose flour

1½ cups/360ml whole milk

5¼ oz/150g cheddar cheese, grated (1⅓ cups)

5¼ oz/150g Red Leicester, grated (1⅓ cups)

a pinch of salt

1 teaspoon cayenne pepper

chopped fresh chives

Makes about 20 **Vegetarian**

These are satisfying to make and incredible to eat and share. Soft, chewy, salty, and delicious, they are boiled (yes, boiled!) and then served with an irresistible cheesy cheese dip.

Start by making the dough. Put the flour and yeast in a bowl with the sugar and mix. Add the butter and rub the butter in till there are no lumps left.

Make a well in the center, add the water, a little at a time (you may not need it all), and bring the dough together. Knead the dough till you have a dough that is smooth and stretchy.

Let rise in a greased bowl till the dough is double the size.

Have two large baking sheets at the ready. Tip out the dough and knead for a few minutes. Make dough balls the size of walnuts. They don't have to be round—misfits and odd shapes are perfect. Pop onto the sheets and let rise, uncovered, for 20 minutes.

Half fill a medium pot with water and add the baking soda. Bring to a boil and let simmer.

Preheat the oven to 375°F.

Take the dough balls and drop into the simmering water for 20 seconds, making sure to turn after 10 seconds. Using a slotted spoon, pop back onto the sheets. Do this to all of the dough balls. Once you have done them all, brush with the egg and sprinkle with flaky salt. Bake for 20–25 minutes.

Meanwhile, make the sauce by putting the butter into a small pot. As soon as the butter has melted, add the flour and mix, then pour in the milk and whisk. On medium heat, whisk till the mixture has thickened.

Take off the heat and add the two cheeses, salt, cayenne, and chives and mix. As soon as the pretzels are out, eat warm with the warm cheese sauce.

ruby eggs

12 large eggs

2 fresh beets

6⅓ cups/1.5 liters cold water

1 tablespoon salt

2 tablespoons apple cider vinegar

1⅔ cups/400ml oil

For the crispy spice coating

¾ cup/100g all-purpose flour

3 tablespoons rice flour

2 teaspoons salt

2 teaspoons cayenne pepper

1 tablespoon dried chives

2 teaspoons onion granules

1 teaspoon garlic powder

1 egg, lightly beaten

| Makes 24 | Vegetarian |

Perfect for a gathering, these look impressive but in fact are the simplest things to make, with the eggs hard-boiled and then left to sit in beet juice. Once they've soaked, they are cut, coated, and baked to create a crisp crunchy exterior. You will love these! You'll find more photos on the next page.

Start by boiling the eggs till they are hard-boiled. Let cool completely, then drain. Now crack but don't peel the shells and set the eggs aside.

Blend the beets and put in a large container with the water, salt, and vinegar. Add the eggs and chill in the fridge for at least 24 hours.

Remove the shells from the eggs and you should have a beautiful purple, marbled, cracked-earth effect. Cut in half lengthwise and set aside.

Preheat the oven to 400°F. Cover a rimmed baking sheet with the oil and pop into the oven.

Mix the flour, rice flour, salt, cayenne, chives, onion, and garlic on a plate. Put the beaten egg on another plate.

Take each egg and dip the flat side into beaten egg to wet a little, then dip into the spiced flour and set aside. Do the same to all of the eggs. Take the hot baking sheet out of the oven and place the eggs flour-side down into the hot oil to bake till crispy.

Bake for 12 minutes. Take out of the oven and let cool completely on the sheet. Remove from the sheet and serve with a simple dip. Soft whites, creamy yolk, and crispy exterior! →

aromatic chicken biryani

Serves 4–6   Gluten-free

For the chicken

7 tablespoons/100ml olive oil

5 cloves of garlic, minced

3 onions, diced

2 teaspoons salt

2 tablespoons tomato paste

3 tablespoons garam masala

1 tablespoon paprika

1 lb/450g diced boneless chicken

2 tablespoons cornstarch

For the rice

1¼ cups/250g basmati rice

3¼ cups/750ml water

1 teaspoon salt

1 large cinnamon stick

a large pinch of saffron strands

To serve

a large bunch of green onions, sliced

lemon and lime wedges

Whether for a midweek dinner, a weekend meal, or a big celebration, biryani is always my go-to. What I'm really saying is that you don't need a reason. With saffron-infused rice and aromatic chicken, this biryani is baked in the oven for ease and left to steam till just perfect.

Preheat the oven to 375°F.

You will need a large Dutch oven with a tight-fitting lid. Put the oil, garlic, onion, salt, tomato paste, garam masala, paprika, and chicken into the pan and mix everything together. Sprinkle with the cornstarch and mix again.

Pop into the oven and bake for 30 minutes.

Meanwhile, make the rice by putting the rice into a pot with the water, salt, cinnamon, and saffron. Bring to a boil and cook for 5 minutes.

Take off the heat and drain in a sieve, running under cold water to prevent the rice grains from sticking.

Now, take the chicken out of the oven and turn the oven off. Add the drained rice on top, cover with foil, and secure with the lid.

Let steam for 20 minutes in the turned-off (but still warm) oven. Take out and give the biryani a mix. Sprinkle the green onions over the top and serve with wedges of lemon and lime.

baked
shrimp toast

Serves 8

I love shrimp toast, so there's not much else to say! This is my take on it: a simple baked shrimp toast that is easy to make and bursting with Thai green curry flavor and fresh shrimp.

oil, for greasing

8 slices of white bread, crusts removed and saved

7 oz/200g raw shrimp, shells and tails removed

2 large eggs

3 tablespoons Thai green curry paste

2 green chiles

a small handful of fresh cilantro

1 tablespoon black sesame seeds

1 tablespoon white sesame seeds

sweet chile sauce, to serve

Get a large baking sheet ready and grease with oil. Preheat the oven to 400°F.

Take the slices of bread and, using a rolling pin, roll the bread flat.

Now, make the shrimp paste. Put the shrimp, eggs, curry paste, half the reserved bread crusts, chiles, and cilantro in a food processor or blender and blitz to a smooth paste.

Transfer to a bowl, add the sesame seeds, and mix well. Now spread the shrimp paste in an even layer onto the flattened bread. Make sure to spread it all the way to the sides.

Pop onto the greased sheet and bake in the oven for 10–12 minutes, till the bread is crisp and the aromatic shrimp are cooked. Cut into triangles and serve hot with sweet chile sauce.

spiced potato puff pastry cups

11¼oz/320g puff pastry, defrosted if frozen

1 egg, lightly beaten

a pinch of salt

For the filling

1 medium potato, peeled, diced, boiled and drained

½ red onion, finely diced

1¼ cups/200g cooked chickpeas, drained

a small handful of fresh cilantro, finely chopped

1 green chile, thinly sliced

a pinch of salt

For the tamarind water

2¼ oz/60g tamarind paste

7 tablespoons/100ml water

½ teaspoon chile powder

½ teaspoon ground cumin

1 teaspoon chaat masala

1 teaspoon ground black pepper

Makes 24   Vegetarian

These are delicious treats that we always eat when we are in Bangladesh. One of the reasons why I love to visit Bangladesh—family aside, of course—is the street food. These crisp little pockets are filled with spiced chickpea and potato, with a spicy tamarind water poured in and knocked right back like a shot. They are not just fun, but delicious too. This recipe is for my cheat's version made with store-bought puff pastry. Kind of like vol-au-vents but Bangladesh style!

Start by making the pastry cases. Preheat the oven to 400°F. Roll the pastry out onto a piece of parchment paper placed on a baking sheet.

Cut 24 equal squares of pastry using a sharp knife or pizza cutter. Take a bottle top and use it to mark each square in the center, then use a knife to score the inside of the round. Don't cut all the way through, just score firmly. Brush with the egg and sprinkle with the salt.

Bake in the oven for 20–25 minutes, till crisp and golden.

Meanwhile, make the filling by mashing the cooked potato using your hands or a fork. Add the onion, chickpeas, cilantro, chile, and salt and mix well. Get your hands in and squeeze enough to break up the chickpeas. Set aside.

Take the pastry out and use a knife to separate the squares. Use the base of the bottle top to push the scored circle into the pastry to create a small cavity for the potato and chickpea mix to sit in. Fill each cavity with the potato mix.

Now, make the tamarind water by putting the tamarind, water, chile, cumin, chaat masala, and black pepper in a small pot and bringing to a boil. Take off the heat and pour into a small vessel with a pouring spout.

To eat, pick up a filled square, pour the spicy tamarind water into the cavity around the potato mix, and get it straight into your mouth!

whole citrus sea bass

oil, for greasing

1 x 1¼–1¾ lb/600–800g sea bass

salt

For the coating

1 orange, juice and zest

1 lime, juice and zest

½ lemon, juice and zest

1 grapefruit, juice only

6 cloves of garlic

1 tablespoon salt

1 teaspoon ground turmeric

1 onion, chopped

1⅔ cups/150g chickpea flour (gram flour), plus a little extra

7 tablespoons/100ml olive oil

To serve

different colored carrots, ribboned

zucchini, ribboned

½ lemon, juice only

olive oil

a pinch of chile flakes

salt and ground black pepper

| Serves 6–8   Gluten-free |

Eating fish and fruit together is in my blood. But mostly it takes place in curry form, so here I wanted to create a recipe that has those familiar flavors but not in a curry. This whole large sea bass is cooked with a citrusy-floured coating that acts like a stuffing when baked. It's perfect served with colorful ribbons of quick-cooked carrots and zucchini. A whole fish cooked at the center of a table screams special occasion.

Start by preheating the oven to 400°F and finding a baking sheet large enough to comfortably fit the very large fish. Trim fins and tail if necessary to make it fit. Lightly grease the entire sheet. On a piece of parchment paper, lightly season the fish with salt inside and out. Dust the fish with some chickpea flour all over and set aside.

Make the coating by combining the orange, lime, lemon, and grapefruit juice and the zest of the orange, lemon, and lime in a blender or food processor. Add the garlic, salt, turmeric, and onion and blitz to a smooth paste.

Transfer to a bowl, tip in the chickpea flour, and mix till you have a mixture that is a smooth paste. Pour in the oil and mix well.

Pop the fish onto the sheet and slash the flesh in a few places to help it cook through. Spread the fish with the delicious paste on both sides. Put into the oven and bake for 45 minutes.

Mix the ribboned vegetables with the lemon, olive oil, and chile flakes and season. Set aside to marinate and soften.

Take the fish out and serve with the ribboned colorful veg. I love the crispy bits of baked citrus batter, a little like stuffing but different, totally delicious alongside the tender sea bass.

chicken shashlik

Serves 4

For the brine

2 tablespoons salt

¼ cup/60ml vinegar

8½ cups/2 liters water

2 lb 2 oz–3⅓ 1 b/
1–1.5kg chicken
thighs

For the marinade

7 tablespoons/100ml
oil

2 tablespoons paprika

¼ cup/55g garlic paste

¼ cup/55g ginger
paste

1 teaspoon salt

¼ cup/65g yogurt

1 cup/100g chickpea
flour (gram flour)

For the vegetables

4 red onions,
quartered

4 yellow bell peppers,
quartered

4 pickled eggs,
halved

3 tablespoons olive oil

1 teaspoon salt

a large handful of
fresh cilantro

To serve

4 naans

chile sauce

This is a meal that my dad served up at his restaurant all day, every day. I've decided to make my own version—tender spiced chicken and roasted veg, all served up with a naan. I don't have a tandoor, but we do have an oven, and with that, a good brine, and a decent marinade, we can make the same thing.

Start by brining the chicken. Put the salt, vinegar, and water in a large bowl. Mix and add the chicken thighs. Cover, set aside, and let brine for 1 hour.

Meanwhile, mix the marinade by putting the oil, paprika, garlic, ginger, salt, yogurt, and chickpea flour in a bowl and whisking till you have a smooth paste.

Now, prep the veg and put the red onion, peppers, and pickled eggs into a roasting pan. Mix well with the oil and salt and set aside.

Once the chicken has been brining for 1 hour, drain and remove any excess brine water.

Preheat the oven to 425°F.

Add the chicken to the bowl with the marinade and mix well. To get a really intense flavor or simply to get ahead, you could do this beforehand and marinate it, covered, in the fridge overnight.

You will need eight skewers. Push a whole chicken thigh onto two skewers, one skewer on each side of the thigh so the meat is spread out. Add more thighs to the same pair of skewers, not too tight together or the meat won't cook through. Repeat with the other skewers and thighs so you have four sets. Lay the skewers horizontally across the roasting pan so they dangle above the vegetables.

Cover with a piece of parchment paper, then foil, and bake for 30 minutes.

Uncover the chicken, remove the foil and paper, and bake for 20 minutes. The chicken should be cooked through with some tasty, charred bits. Take the chicken off the skewers and slice.

Sprinkle cilantro over the vegetables and mix. Get some warm naan, fill with the hot veg and sliced chicken, drizzle with some good chile sauce, and enjoy.

Sicilian meatloaf

For the meatloaf

1 tablespoon olive oil, plus extra for greasing

3 cloves of garlic, minced

1¼ cups/100g crispy fried onions

2 tablespoons tomato paste

1 tablespoon yeast extract

1 medium potato, grated

1 medium carrot, grated

3 tablespoons chickpea flour (gram flour)

1 lb 2 oz/500g ground turkey

1 teaspoon salt

3 tablespoons ketchup

3 tablespoons steak sauce

For the butter beans

drizzle of olive oil

2 x 15-oz/425g cans of butter beans (fava beans), drained

1 x 14-oz/400g can of cream of tomato soup

1 teaspoon chile flakes

1 teaspoon garlic powder

1 teaspoon salt

balsamic vinegar

a large handful of fresh parsley

> **Serves 6   Gluten-free**

Meatloaf is one of my favorite meals to make and eat with the family, but its simplicity can mean it often gets filed among mid-week meals and overlooked for special occasions. But a good meatloaf, flavored well, really can take center stage; it, too, can dazzle and be the belle of the ball! This meatloaf is moist, lightly spiced, and sits on a bed of tomatoey butter beans, perfect for any celebration.

Heat the oven to 400°F and have a 9 x 5-inch/900g loaf pan greased and ready and also a large roasting pan.

Start by making the meatloaf mix. Put the olive oil, garlic, onions, tomato paste, and yeast extract in a bowl. Add the potato, carrot, chickpea flour, ground turkey, and salt. Get your hands in and mix well. In handfuls, fill the loaf pan and pack in tightly.

Into the roasting pan put the oil, butter beans, tomato soup, chile, garlic, and salt and mix.

Pop the meatloaf on the top oven rack and the butter beans underneath and bake for 30 minutes.

Once the meatloaf is cooked and the beans have roasted and warmed through, take both of them out of the oven. Remove the meatloaf from the pan and place right on top of the beans.

Mix the ketchup and steak sauce, spread all over the meatloaf, and bake for 5 minutes, till the top of the meatloaf is toasted. Take out and drizzle with balsamic. Sprinkle with the parsley and mix well. It is ready to eat. Center stage!

gulab jamun cheesecake

Serves 8–10   Vegetarian

For the crust

8 oz/225g graham crackers

7 tablespoons/100g unsalted butter, melted, plus extra for greasing

For the filling

1 cup plus 2 tablespoons/250g mascarpone

1 lb 5 oz/600g full-fat cream cheese

2 large eggs, plus 2 large egg yolks

¼ cup/30g all-purpose flour

¾ cup plus 2 tablespoons/175g sugar

4 cardamom pods

2 x 1 lb 2 oz/500g packages of gulab jamun in syrup (12 balls total)

¾ cup/100g pistachios, roughly chopped

This is a combination of two things that I really love. Gulab jamun is a ball of cake dough that is deep-fried till dark golden and then dunked into a sweet syrup and left to soak up all that syrupy goodness. Meanwhile, my favorite kind of cheesecake is that of the baked variety. So, I decided it was time to put them together—the dense richness of baked cheesecake spiked with the sweetness of a syrupy cake.

Start by greasing and lining the bottom and sides of a 9-inch/23cm springform round cake pan. Preheat the oven to 350°F.

Crush the graham crackers till you have a fine, even crumb. Add the melted butter to the graham cracker crumbs and mix till you have a mixture that looks like wet sand. Tip into the bottom of the pan and, using the back of a spoon, compress the mixture, packing down as tightly as possible.

Now, make the filling by mixing the mascarpone, cream cheese, eggs, egg yolks, flour, and sugar really well. Break the cardamom pods, take out the little seeds, and crush to a fine powder. Add to the mixture and combine.

Drain the gulab jamun balls, take each sweet ball into your hands, and squeeze as much syrupy juice as possible out. Place the balls into the bottom of the pan on top of the graham cracker crumb.

Pour in the cheesecake mixture. Sprinkle with the pistachios and bake in the oven for 40–45 minutes, till the center is just a little bit wobbly.

Turn the oven off and allow the cheesecake to cool completely in the oven. When cool, put the cheesecake in the fridge to chill for a minimum of 4 hours and at best overnight. Take out, remove the pan, and cut into wedges. To serve the cheesecake, I love to drizzle some sweet rose syrup over the top.

meringue cake

Serves 6   Vegetarian

For the cake batter

½ cup/125g unsalted butter, softened

½ cup/ 100g granulated sugar

4 large egg yolks

1 cup/125g all-purpose flour

1 teaspoon baking powder

1 teaspoon vanilla extract

2 tablespoons whole milk

For the meringue

4 large egg whites

1 teaspoon cream of tartar

1 cup/200g granulated sugar

For the filling

1¼ cups/300ml heavy cream

2 tablespoons confectioners' sugar

1¼ cups/150g berries, chopped

1 lemon, finely grated zest only

cocoa powder, for dusting (optional)

If you are looking for a simple, light cake, this is the one for you. Two layers of meringue are baked on the thinnest layers of sponge cake, then sandwiched with fresh cream and fruit. Pillowy light but still so satisfying.

Grease and line two 8-inch/20cm cake pans. Preheat the oven to 400°F.

Start by making the cake batter. Put the butter, sugar, egg yolks, flour, baking powder, vanilla, and milk in a bowl and mix till you have a smooth paste.

Divide the mixture between the two pans and use an offset spatula to spread into a thin, even layer on the bottom of each pan. It doesn't look like much, but this very thin layer of cake will make a whole lot of difference to the light meringue.

Now, set aside while you make the meringue. Put the egg whites in a clean bowl with the cream of tartar. Whisk till they start to become frothy. Add the sugar, one spoonful at a time, making sure to incorporate each addition and allowing the sugar to dissolve in. Keep adding till there is no sugar left.

Divide the mixture between the two pans, smoothing it down so it sits flush on top of the cake batter. Flatten the top of one and make peaks on the other.

Bake in the oven for 20–25 minutes, till golden on top. If the meringue looks like it's browning too fast, lower the oven temperature a little toward the end of the cooking time. Take out of the oven and let cool in the pans completely. Once cool, take the flatter meringue out of its pan and place on a serving dish, cake-side down.

Whip the cream with the confectioners' sugar till just thickened and holding soft peaks. Add two-thirds of the chopped berries and lemon zest and fold them in. Top the meringue and spread the fruity cream all over in an even layer. Dot the rest of the berries onto it.

Now, top with the other meringue, cake-side down and peaks at the top. Dust with a little cocoa, if you like, and you are ready to eat this pillowy-light, delicious meringue-layer cake.

celebration days

garden of Eden blondies

| Makes 9 | Vegetarian |

For the blondies

¾ cup/175g unsalted butter, plus extra for greasing

1½ cups/300g sugar

3 large eggs

1 teaspoon vanilla extract

1 teaspoon almond extract

1½ cups/200g all-purpose flour

¾ cup/100g macadamia nuts, roughly chopped

For the top

7 oz/200g white chocolate

herb leaves

edible flowers

Blondies are for those of us who have a sweet tooth and are not wedded to the idea that everything delicious must have chocolate in it. I mean, all things chocolate are delicious, but these sweet, dense blondies are delicious too. But just to keep the chocoholics happy as well, I have finished these off with a drizzle of caramelized white chocolate with a beautiful garden of herbs and fresh flowers set into it.

Grease and line an 8-inch/20cm square cake pan.

Melt the butter and let cool. Put the sugar and eggs in a bowl and whisk till light and fluffy. This should take 5 minutes and the mixture will have tripled in size.

Now, add the vanilla, almond, and cooled melted butter and mix well. Add the flour and mix till you have an even batter.

Pour into and level off in the cake pan. Chill the batter in the fridge for 40 minutes.

Preheat the oven to 325°F.

As soon as the oven comes to temperature, sprinkle the batter with the macadamias and bake for 50–60 minutes. Once out of the oven, let cool in the pan completely and as soon as it does, if you can bear it, chill overnight and this will not only give you an easier straight cut into the blondies, but you will get a fudgier texture.

Now, melt the chocolate and pour or drizzle all over in an even layer. Carefully add the flowers and herbs and allow to set again in the fridge.

Take out and use a sharp knife dipped in hot water to cut even, straight squares. Pile up and plough into your garden of Eden.

angel layer cake slices

Serves 8–10   **Vegetarian**

For the cake

1 cup plus
2 tablespoons/250g unsalted butter, softened, plus extra for greasing the pan

1¼ cups/250g granulated sugar

5 large eggs

2 cups/250g all-purpose flour, sifted

½ teaspoon vanilla extract

½ teaspoon almond extract

a few drops of pink gel food coloring

For the icing

1⅔ cups/200g fondant icing sugar or confectioners' sugar

2–3 tablespoons water

pink and yellow gel food coloring

Oh, my goodness, angel layer cake was my go-to when I was younger and had a few extra pennies. I would take myself to the corner shop and buy those familiar branded packages of apple pies and angel cake slices. I still love the subtle colors and flavors of this cake and I wanted to create a homemade version, but I think the idea of baking multiple layers can be daunting, so I've devised a simple recipe that gives us layers without needing separate pans. Hardly any of the work but all of the beauty.

Preheat the oven to 375°F and grease and line a 9 x 13-inch/23 x 33cm baking pan.

Start by putting the butter and sugar in a bowl and beating till the mixture is light and creamy. Add the eggs in, one by one, till each one is incorporated well. Add the flour and mix for 2 minutes, till you have a smooth batter.

Add half the batter into the bottom of the cake pan and level off into a thin layer. Give the pan a few sharp taps to really level off the surface and remove any air bubbles.

To the rest of the batter, add the vanilla and almond extracts and a few drops of the pink food coloring and mix till it's an even pink color. Spoon into a piping bag.

Pipe evenly over the white cake layer and spread gently to level off the top, making sure not to ripple or mix with the batter underneath. Tap the pan a few times on the work surface to release any air bubbles.

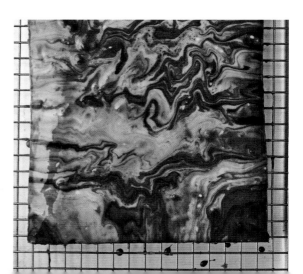

Bake for 30 minutes. Take out and let cool in the pan for 15 minutes before transferring onto a cooling rack to cool completely.

Put the fondant icing sugar in a bowl with the water and keep mixing till you have a thick mixture that drips slowly and coats the back of a spoon.

Pop a drop of yellow food coloring onto one side and pink on the other, leaving the middle bit white. Using a skewer, mix in each of the colors, keeping them as separate as possible. Set something under-neath the cooling rack to catch the excess icing.

Pour the mixture onto the cake and see what happens—you should see the colors blend and swirl to make a mesmerizing, colored pattern. Once the icing has stopped running, pop onto a serving dish and slice up your simple angel cake.

acknowledgments

Thank you to everyone involved in helping to bring this book together. A job bigger than you might imagine, but without the hard work of these people we would never end up with this book.

Thank you to Georgia for testing all the recipes, for enjoying them, for the feedback.

Thank you to Chris Terry for being the best at what he does and taking beautiful pictures of the food and, dare I say, me!

Thank you to Rob, Hollie, and Ayala for all the work on creating the recipes so they are shoot ready.

Thank you, Roya, for making everything look exactly as it should; it always looks like I imagined it in my mind.

Thank you, Sarah, for literally wrapping everything in your beautiful vision.

Thank you, Heather, for always making me feel like a million dollars. You are much more than makeup— you make up bits of me that the camera does not see.

Thank you, Anne, for always starting every sentence with "can we eat that now?"

Thank you, Dan and Ione, for being there from the baby step stages, to the relay running and all the way to the finish line.

Thank you to the entire MJ team, including Aggie, Bea, Dan P-B, Alice, Gaby, Sophie, Catherine, and Anjali, for being a part of a huge project of which none of it would be possible without your hard work.

Thank you to my little team, Abdal, Musa, Dawud, Maryam, and not forgetting my beautiful sub-team Shak, Sara, Sulayman, and Noor, for getting through the cake!

index

CLARKSON POTTER is a trademark
and POTTER with colophon is a
registered trademark of Penguin
Random House LLC.

Originally published in hardcover in
Great Britain by Michael Joseph, a
division of Penguin Random House
Ltd., London, in 2022. By arrangement
with the BBC.

Library of Congress Cataloging-
in-Publication Data is available.

ISBN 978-0-593-57905-3
Ebook ISBN 978-0-593-57906-0

Printed in Canada

10 9 8 7 6 5 4 3 2 1

First American Edition